TA IN CONTROL

SMASHING TIME!

A TEACHING ASSISTANTS' PLANNER THAT SHOWS YOU HOW TO MAKE MORE TIME IN A JOB WHERE EVERYTHING NEEDS TO BE DONE YESTERDAY!

ABOUT SMASHING TIME!

Smashing Time is a Time Planner and Journal rolled into one. It helps Teaching Assistants (TAs) prioritise your time and your workload as well as making MORE of your time!

Schools are difficult places to work for many reasons but this book will focus on just 2 of those reasons:

1. There is always too much to do.
2. There is always too little time to do it in.

Having been a TA/HLTA/1:1 TA for 20 years I know first-hand how exhausting and relentless the role of TA is. It wasn't like that when I first became a TA though. Back in the late 90's/early 2000's I definitely remember feeling a sense of job satisfaction. A sense of doing my job well and sense of enjoyment at the thought of another day at school.

But when I left my last school, all of that had gone. It had been replaced with a frustrated feeling of being used for whatever was necessary, including washing dishes and following children who didn't want to be at school, around the school all day!

For me though, part of my unhappiness was led by my body having moved into the menopause and, like many women at this stage of life, I began to feel that my internal changes were telling me that change was also needed externally. So, I left, abruptly with 2 days' notice! I was free!

Two years later, and here I am writing books for TAs, running a membership for Teaching Assistants to fix their defeating thoughts and managing social media, to name just a few of the things that keep me busy each day.

I'm doing this because I believe that TAs make a HUGE difference to the lives of the children they support and whilst I'd had enough of school myself, I still want to show TAs that being a Teaching Assistant IS a GREAT job...when you work at your most confident best!

At my last count I had around 32 planners, journals, notebooks and diaries published on Amazon. They're all made specifically to support TAs in your work, and this book about time, is my 33rd. I am writing it because 'more time' is the number one thing TAs say would make your lives less stressful.

But, I'm not at all sure that you REALLY want MORE time. What I believe you want is less stuff packed into your time. I believe you want a sense of using your time well and along with that a sense that you can, once again, enjoy the time you spend at school.

So, 'Smashing Time' isn't just about smashing through your issues about time, it's also about regaining a sense of HAVING a 'smashing' time at school, as in enjoying being a Teaching Assistant. And I see no reason for this to be an unobtainable goal, especially for those of you who want to make the role of TA work for you and your family life.

But it might require some flexibility in your thinking and the willingness to move away from what you believe to be true, so that you move towards a new perspective of what it means to be a Teaching Assistant in the 2020s.

And it might require some flexibility about the way you perceive time because we humans have the ability to do so much more with time than our linear (clock time) understanding of it would have us believe!

ABOUT TIME & SMASHING IT!

There is a growing body of research to show that other creatures, be it insects, mammals, birds, reptiles etc, perceive time differently to humans. We know, for instance, that small animals who are the prey of other animals can see an approaching predator at a slower pace than we can, enabling it to make a quick getaway. You only have to think of an annoying housefly for proof of this. How DOES it evade your rolled up newspaper so brilliantly?!

Time, as we humans know it i.e. 24 hours in a day, 60 minutes to every hour etc, is a man-made concept. No other creature on this earth experiences time in the way we do. Your dog or cat does not wake up in the morning and think 'Sh*t, I'm late! I'll never get ready in 10 minutes!'

Eminent scientists such as Albert Einstein, Sir Isaac Newton and many more have differing theories on what time actually is beyond linear clock time. When you think about it, most of us have experienced days when time has appeared to go slower or faster than expected.

We've all had conversations about time dragging. In my experience this happened most frequently in English lessons when Year 3 children were tasked with adding embedded clauses to their sentences. OMG... time seemed to slow down 10 fold in those lessons!

And we've all had conversations about time flying by. Break times, when I wasn't on playground duty, would always go much more quickly it seemed to me!

Our perception of time can be different depending on how positively or negatively we feel about what we are experiencing, with positive experiences passing more rapidly than negative ones.

I'm sure you've experienced a lesson where you've felt particularly inspired, confident and organised, and you've been surprised when a student has asked what the time is. You can't believe you only have another 20 minutes left but the student complains about how slowly the lesson is going.

Clock time has been the same for both of you, but your perception of time has been different. Your POSITIVE experience indicates you were in something called 'flow state' otherwise known as 'in the zone' but the bored student, wasn't!

Why am I saying all of this? Well, really because I want you to see your reason for buying this book from more than one perspective. Whilst we will look at practical ways for you to fit everything you need to do into the time you have, I also want to show you ways to enter FLOW STATE more often so that you make your EXPERIENCE of time more ENJOYABLE.

If you can add more enjoyable experiences of time into your day, your days will become more enjoyable. As your days become more enjoyable your experiences of FLOW STATE will increase, giving you a sense of time EXPANDING. And with that sense of time EXPANDING, you REALLY WILL feel as though you are MAKING more time.

So, whilst it isn't possible to make more LINEAR (CLOCK) time – because, with the way we currently measure time, there can only EVER BE 24 hours in a day, it is possible to change our PERCEPTION of time by INCREASING our POSITIVE experiences and DECREASING our NEGATIVE experiences.

This change in your perception of time depending on your frame of reference i.e. whether or not you are enjoying yourself, Einstein called, RELATIVITY.

Use this book to explore different ways of making MORE TIME by way of CLOCK-TIME methods and RELATIVE-TIME methods.

With each method, you'll also have an opportunity to write down your experience of it and reflect on how you can use it to improve your experience as a Teaching Assistant.

'Not possible!' I hear you cry...

This is the voice in your head that resists anything different from what you believe to be true. So, if you are hearing that voice right now and experiencing the feeling of resistance, put it to one side. Treat it like you would any child in school who is reluctant to learn something new.

At the very least this book will teach you <u>one</u> way of making time work better for you and at the very best it will teach you many ways of doing that. If your experience of this book falls between the least and the best, then you will have learned several ways of making time work better for you.

Even if you have the least experience, one is still better than none. But if you do what you encourage your students to do, namely – do the work – you will find more than one way to make more time.

As with ALL of my TA IN CONTROL books, a certain amount of work is required from you. I cannot make the words inside this book jump out and assimilate into your brain and into your working life. Only YOU can do that!

Is saying you want more time merely an idle wish? Or do you intend to do something about it?

"WE CANNOT SOLVE OUR PROBLEMS WITH THE SAME THINKING WE USED WHEN WE CREATED THEM."

ALBERT EINSTEIN

TA IN CONTROL

YOU'LL FIND ALL
OF YOUR
ANSWERS
WHEN
SOMEBODY
ASKS YOU THE
RIGHT QUESTIONS!

VALUE:

the regard that something is held to deserve; the importance, worth, or usefulness of something.

HOW MUCH DO YOU VALUE YOUR TIME?

You will never know the answer to something if you are not asked a question about it. So, in this section of SMASHING TIME I will ask some questions about the following aspects of YOUR TIME:

- Valuing time as a commodity you <u>sell</u> to your school.

- Valuing time as a commodity you <u>give for free</u> to your school.

- Valuing time as a commodity you give to yourself.

- Valuing time as a commodity you give to family & friends.

Notice the language I am using. It's all positive. None of this is about downgrading anything. It's about valuing and prioritising everything that is important to you.

And once you've gone through the exercises in this book you'll have worked out exactly what you value and want to prioritise most in your life. In this way, you'll get the sense of always having enough time rather than feeling like time is a scarce resource.

VALUING TIME AS A COMMODITY YOU <u>SELL</u> TO YOUR SCHOOL.

THINK ABOUT IT! Time is your MOST PRECIOUS COMMODITY because no amount of money will buy you more time.

Not even the RICHEST PERSON in the WORLD can create more than 24 hours in a day for themselves. In this way YOU and the richest person are the same!

NO ONE has MORE than 24 hours in a day. NO ONE can stop time from marching forward. EVERY day that passes is a day you will NEVER get back!

We ALL enter this world with a certain TIME ALLOWANCE, but NONE of us are born knowing how much time we've been given and whether our time will be cut short!

And this is why it is <u>so important</u> that you appreciate the time you have SO MUCH that you DO NOT give it away FREELY...UNLESS...you GENUINELY WANT TO.

When you sign a job contract you are essentially saying that you will fulfil the terms of the contract in return for the agreed amount of money. You are agreeing to work X number of hours for X amount of money.

Being a TA unfortunately requires you to accept a low amount of money for your time. Now, this is unlikely to change any time soon AND there will, no doubt, be advantages to being a TA, that make it work for you and your family.

HOWEVER, the first thing you need to UNDERSTAND is that YOUR TIME is <u>YOUR</u> TIME. You have agreed to SELL it for whatever your TA salary is. THOSE hours and only THOSE are being paid for by your school.

There is <u>NOTHING</u> in your contract that says, 'Oo, but if you come in early or stay late, of course, we'll respect the fact you are using YOUR precious time allowance, and pay you!'

In fact, it's EXACTLY the opposite because many TAs sign your job contract, that agrees you'll work a certain number of hours for a certain amount of money, but at some point you say 'Oo, but I'll come in early and I'll stay late and use my precious time allowance WITHOUT being paid!'

VALUING TIME AS A COMMODITY YOU <u>SELL</u> TO YOUR SCHOOL.

In this way you are NOT RESPECTING your own TIME ALLOWANCE. On some level you ARE AWARE of this and this awareness shows up in you as symptoms of stress, anxiety, tiredness and constantly wishing you had MORE TIME!

So, the first exercise I want you to do involves knowing how much you are paid per hour when you work your contracted time and how much you are ACTUALLY being paid per hour when you factor in the TOTAL amount of time you spend at school and on school work at home.

This is about you SEEING EXACTLY what you are doing so that you can decide if this is something you want to continue with or not.

Please understand that I AM NOT JUDGING YOU! I have written this book to help YOU DECIDE how to progress with your work life and family life. If YOU are HAPPY, I'M HAPPY!

But, I'm guessing you're NOT TOTALLY happy with the way you spend your time, or else you wouldn't have bought this book, so doing this exercise will give you VALUABLE information to base your future decisions on.

VALUING TIME AS A COMMODITY YOU <u>SELL</u> TO YOUR SCHOOL.

EXERCISE 1 – WHAT IS YOUR TIME ACTUALLY WORTH?

How many hours are you contracted to work?_____

What is your hourly rate of pay?   _____

How do you feel about this rate of pay?

_____

_____

Calculate how many hours, on average, you work per week <u>including</u> extra hours at school and school work you bring home: _____

Now calculate your ACTUAL hourly rate based on your above answer - READ BELOW TO FIND OUT HOW

HOW TO CALCULATE YOUR ACTUAL HOURLY RATE:

Multiply your contracted hourly rate by the amount of contracted hours you work E.G. £9.75 X 30 HOURS = £292.50 (use the calculator on your phone if this makes your head spin!)

Now divide 292.50 by the ACTUAL number of hours you work each week E.G. £292.50 ÷ 35 = £8.35

Your ACTUAL hourly rate which includes the extra hours you work unpaid, is: _____

VALUING TIME AS A COMMODITY YOU <u>SELL</u> TO YOUR SCHOOL.

EXERCISE 1 - WHAT IS YOUR TIME ACTUALLY WORTH? (CONT'D)

As a point of reference, the National Living Wage from April 2022 for people aged 23 and over is £9.50

How do you feel about your revised hourly rate of pay?

_____

_____

_____

However you feel about it, is fine. Just leave it here for now. We will pick it up again later...

On the next few pages we will explore the concept of valuing time as a commodity you give for free to your school...

VALUING TIME AS A COMMODITY YOU GIVE FOR FREE TO YOUR SCHOOL.

REMEMBER! Our frame of reference THROUGHOUT THIS BOOK is from the point of view that YOUR TIME IS A PRECIOUS COMMODITY YOU CANNOT MAKE MORE OF. It's important you remember this as we explore how YOU use your time...

I am not criticising working for free. I've worked many free hours over my time as a TA and loved every minute of most of them. And the thing is, I never moaned about not having enough time, until I began to resent working for free.

Until resentment kicked in, working for free was about doing more of something I loved and I did not expect the school to pay me for more hours than my contract outlined, unless they'd agreed to it first.

At the time, I believed all of the free hours I did was experience that would pave the way for me to become a Teacher. And in 2006, after gaining a degree, I embarked on my post graduate year of teacher training. I hated it, though, and 6 weeks later went back to my TA role.

So, looking back, I could think that all that free work

was wasted, but hindsight isn't much use in this type of situation.

With that said, YOU need to work out how much of your working day you are happy to give freely. What I mean by that is, what amount of time are you willing to give for free on a regular basis that will fulfil what you believe your school expects of you and what you expect of yourself?

Alternatively, you need to work out if you are happy to give your time for free at all. Many TAs do not work for free. They start their day at their contracted time and they end their day at their contracted time. What stops you from doing this too?

It's probable you do not need to be giving as much free time as you are currently. I'm guessing that the amount of free work you've given your school has crept up over time because that is what happens when you have a belief about your school's expectations of you.

Your belief gets bigger and bigger and it feels like you have to keep adding to it in order to continue fulfilling it!

One thing that allows other TAs to only work the time

VALUING TIME AS A COMMODITY YOU GIVE FOR FREE TO YOUR SCHOOL.

they are paid for is their belief that they are enough.

Because of this belief, they do not need to prove their worth. Most of them don't have thoughts of senior management not renewing their contract because they do not work for free. And those TAs who think not having their contract renewed could be a possibility, also believe they'll find another job because they know their worth.

So, now it's time for another exercise. If you are going to give your school some of your time free of charge, you need to VALUE that time and give it HAPPILY.

Anything LESS than that will create resentment within you which will lead to feelings of frustration, stress, anxiety, tiredness and CONSTANTLY wishing you had MORE TIME!

REMEMBER, doing the following exercise will give you VALUABLE information to base future decisions on...

VALUING TIME AS A COMMODITY YOU GIVE FOR FREE TO YOUR SCHOOL.

EXERCISE 2 – WHAT AMOUNT OF TIME CAN YOU GIVE FREELY & WITH A SENSE OF VALUE AND HAPPINESS?

Simply ask yourself this question:

Now that I know how many free hours I give to my school and what my hourly rate of pay is when I take them into account, what amount of free hours now feels comfortable to me? _____ free hours

Now check in with yourself by asking this question:

When I think about doing the amount of free hours I've just written down, how does that make me feel?

Write down your HONEST response to this question by tapping into the first FEELING you felt when you asked it:

_____

_____

_____

VALUING TIME AS A COMMODITY YOU GIVE FOR FREE TO YOUR SCHOOL.

EXERCISE 2 – WHAT AMOUNT OF TIME CAN YOU GIVE FREELY & WITH A SENSE OF VALUE AND HAPPINESS? (CONT'D)

If the first feeling you felt was a positive one then go ahead with the amount of free hours you've decided upon. We will work on how and when you fit them into your day later on.

If your first feeling was a negative one and particularly if you felt a drain in your energy when you asked it or a dragging sensation, reduce the amount of hours until you feel more positive: _____ free hours

Do not panic if no amount of hours feels good to you or more hours feels good. These exercises are allowing you to gather information that you would not have if you had not asked yourself these questions. Focusing on the free hours you give to your school and being fully conscious about your feelings is a GOOD thing because...

These exercises are helping you gather VALUABLE information to base FUTURE decisions on.

Next, we are going to explore time as a commodity you give to yourself...

VALUING TIME AS A COMMODITY YOU GIVE TO YOURSELF.

For you to improve your expectations in work and life in general you MUST change your belief that YOU come LAST.

When there is an emergency on an aeroplane and the oxygen masks drop down, the instruction for any adult who has children with them is, to use the oxygen mask FIRST because an adult unconscious on the floor is of no use to a child!

Giving EVERYTHING you have to EVERYONE ELSE is an OUTDATED model of womanhood and it leaves you exhausted and not anywhere near your BEST!

It came about through the control of women by men and men's need to be waited on at home while they went about their 'business'.

Giving EVERYTHING you have to EVERYONE ELSE is COMPLETELY unsustainable and leads to you feeling tired, frustrated, resentful, anxious and CONSTANTLY wishing you had MORE TIME!

It's time to STOP making EXCUSES about this one. I hear them time and time again when I coach TAs about their mindset. 'Oh, but if I don't do it, who will?' they say.

VALUING TIME AS A COMMODITY YOU GIVE TO YOURSELF.

'I do it for the children' ; 'Life is just easier if I do it', are two more justifications I hear for taking on TOO MUCH.

If you do not VALUE YOURSELF, NO ONE ELSE WILL.

A woman who VALUES HERSELF, however, teaches others to VALUE her through her own example. As soon as a woman who VALUES herself says 'no' to a request or places a limit on the help she gives, the person making the request feels less able to pass more STUFF in her direction.

The OPPOSITE is true for a woman who does NOT value herself. Every time she says 'yes' she is giving permission for yet MORE STUFF to come her way.

This is NOT about being SELFISH. It's about having some SELF-RESPECT and NOT playing the MARTYR!

It's time to STOP wearing your MARTYRDOM like a BADGE OF HONOUR.

YOU have SO MUCH MORE to give the world than THAT!

YOU have SO MUCH MORE to give the world than THAT!

VALUING TIME AS A COMMODITY YOU GIVE TO YOURSELF.

EXERCISE 3 – WHAT GIFTS DO YOU BRING TO THE WORLD AND HOW MUCH TIME WILL YOU GIVE TO THEM?

When you answer the following questions, write down the first thing that springs to mind. DO NOT CENSOR yourself because you believe you are being unrealistic or for any other reason.

QUESTION 1: Do you believe that the only thing you have to give the world is your complete and utter selflessness? Yes or No? _____

If your answer is 'Yes', park it to one side and carry on...

QUESTION 2: What other gifts do you bring to the world other than selflessness?

Even if you answered yes to question 1, write down some of your abilities that benefit others – you have space for 10 but write at least 5.

1 _____

2 _____

3 _____

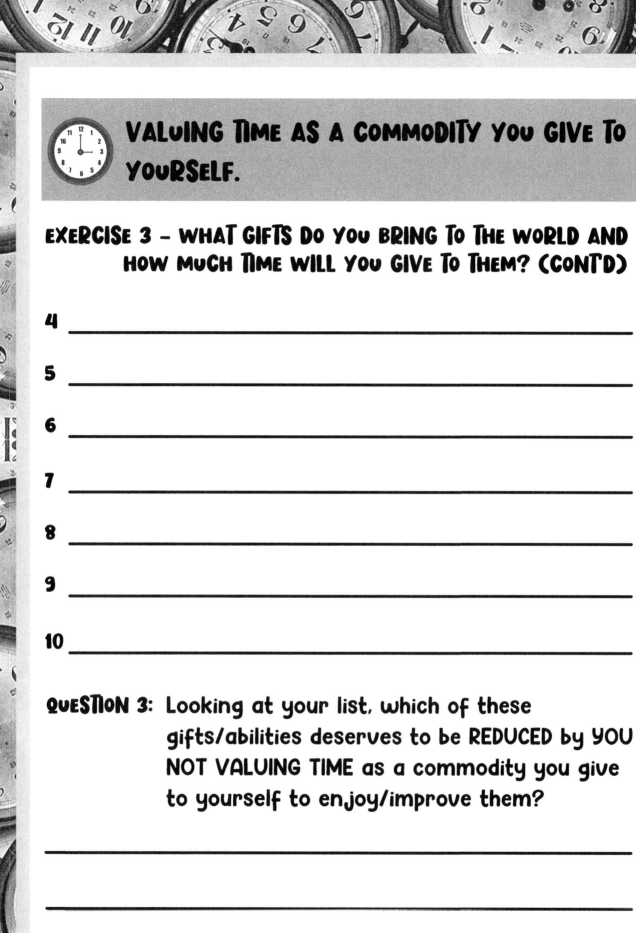

VALUING TIME AS A COMMODITY YOU GIVE TO YOURSELF.

EXERCISE 3 - WHAT GIFTS DO YOU BRING TO THE WORLD AND HOW MUCH TIME WILL YOU GIVE TO THEM? (CONT'D)

4 _____

5 _____

6 _____

7 _____

8 _____

9 _____

10 _____

QUESTION 3: Looking at your list, which of these gifts/abilities deserves to be REDUCED by YOU NOT VALUING TIME as a commodity you give to yourself to enjoy/improve them?

_____

_____

VALUING TIME AS A COMMODITY YOU GIVE TO YOURSELF.

EXERCISE 3 – WHAT GIFTS DO YOU BRING TO THE WORLD AND HOW MUCH TIME WILL YOU GIVE TO THEM? (CONT'D)

I hope you've not been able to bring yourself to write anything other than 'NONE' to the last question but if this is not the case, answer this question:

QUESTION 4: What good comes from reducing them?

_____

_____

QUESTION 5: Looking at your list of gifts you bring to the world, how much time would you like in your day to focus on at least one of them?

_____

DO NOT THINK about how realistic the amount of time you've chosen is, just go with your instinct because...

These exercises are helping you gather VALUABLE information to base FUTURE decisions on.

Next we will explore valuing time as a commodity you give to family and friends...

VALUING TIME AS A COMMODITY YOU GIVE TO FAMILY & FRIENDS.

How important are your family and/or friends to you?

Your answer to this will rely on so many variables that this book does not cover but if you are like most women I know, whose lives are pretty standard, you'll have a well-anchored inner belief that your family is very important, no matter how much stress the individuals in it give you. And you may feel similarly about some of your friends, depending on how close you are.

If you have children, then your feelings about family will be influenced by how well you took to motherhood, whether that was through giving birth to your children, adoption, via surrogacy, taking on children from relatives, being a step-parent etc. Becoming a Mum is certainly one of the hardest things I've ever done!

For me, I think the difficulty was wrapped up in the fact I'd been an only child to loving parents, so I was used to my needs being put first. This, of course, changed once I gave birth to my first child and although I was mature enough at 31 to understand my baby needed love and attention 24/7, the adjustment was still a shock!

VALUING TIME AS A COMMODITY YOU GIVE TO FAMILY & FRIENDS.

Looking back, I wasn't always the Mum I would have liked to have been, but I know I did the best I could with who I was at the time and, happily, I have a great relationship with both my children, who are now 27 and 24. I hope it is the same for you if you are reading this at a later stage of parenthood.

There is, however, something I know now that would have been useful to me back then when I was navigating parenthood as well as other family issues like caring for my own parents, living with in-laws, the expectation family members put on me, as well as the expectations of friends, and that something is this...

I am NOT my family and I am NOT my friends.

Being a family member or part of a friendship group is NOT like swimming in the sea as part of a shoal of fish or flying in the sky as part of a murmuration of birds.

This means that I and YOU do not have to ALTER course as soon as someone in the family or friendship group goes OFF course.

It may require an adjustment or two, depending on the situation but it DOESN'T HAVE TO MEAN that you lose

VALUING TIME AS A COMMODITY YOU GIVE TO FAMILY & FRIENDS.

sight of WHO you are, WHERE you are and WHERE you WANT TO BE.

So, if you are feeling like your family and/or friends take up too much of your time, leaving you no time for yourself, you need to understand that being part of a family and/or friendship group is NOT the TOTALITY of WHO you are.

Being part of a family and/or friendship group SHOULD in the main, ENHANCE your life rather than SUCK the life out of it.

Exercise 3, 'Valuing Time As a Commodity You Give to Yourself', plays a part in this. If YOU are getting ENOUGH time for YOU, you are MORE LIKELY to ENJOY your family and friends. YOU were not put on this Earth to be at the beck and call of others and believing that you ARE AT THE BECK AND CALL OF OTHERS will only put a strain on your relationships.

In Exercise 4 we will take what you have learned from Exercise 3 and enhance it by finding out what you enjoy about being with family and friends, what you feel you MUST do for them and what you feel you can LET GO of.

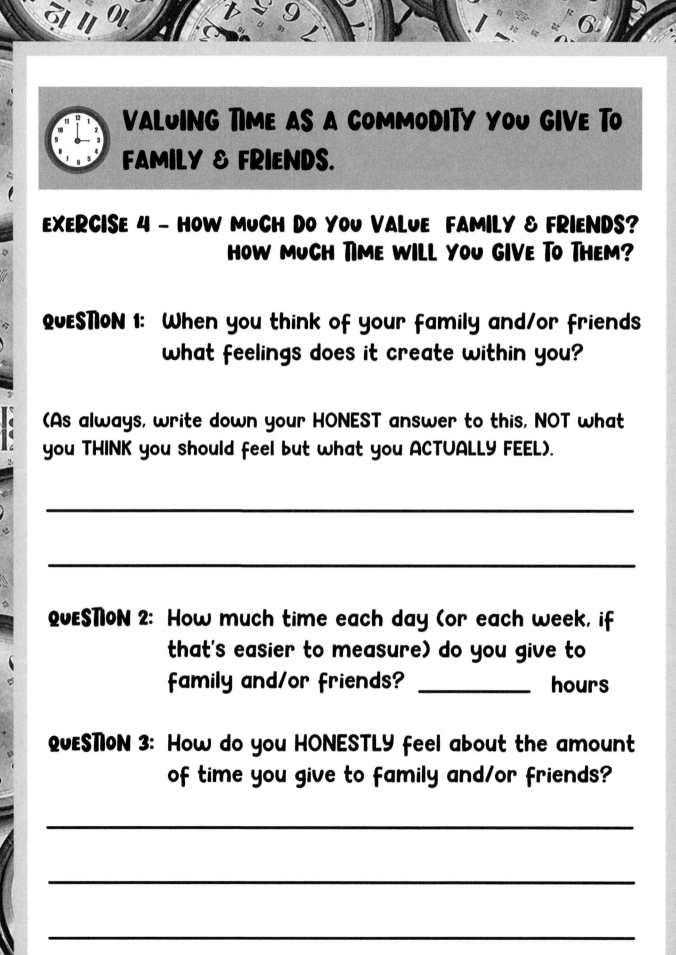

VALUING TIME AS A COMMODITY YOU GIVE TO FAMILY & FRIENDS.

EXERCISE 4 – HOW MUCH DO YOU VALUE FAMILY & FRIENDS? HOW MUCH TIME WILL YOU GIVE TO THEM?

QUESTION 1: When you think of your family and/or friends what feelings does it create within you?

(As always, write down your HONEST answer to this, NOT what you THINK you should feel but what you ACTUALLY FEEL).

_____

_____

QUESTION 2: How much time each day (or each week, if that's easier to measure) do you give to family and/or friends? _____ hours

QUESTION 3: How do you HONESTLY feel about the amount of time you give to family and/or friends?

_____

_____

_____

VALUING TIME AS A COMMODITY YOU GIVE TO FAMILY & FRIENDS.

EXERCISE 4 – HOW MUCH DO YOU VALUE FAMILY & FRIENDS? HOW MUCH TIME WILL YOU GIVE TO THEM? (CONT'D)

QUESTION 4: How much time per day or week would you LIKE to give to family and/or friends?

_____ hours

QUESTION 5: From the time you already give to family and/or friends, how much of that time is taken up with NON ESSENTIAL things?

_____ hours

To help you work this out: Is it essential YOU do something or could someone else do it? Is it essential that your children do 4 afterschool activities or could that be reduced to 3? I'm asking you here to REALLY THINK about the expectations you believe others have of you that really stem from the unrealistic expectations you put on yourself.

QUESTION 6: From the time you already give to family and/or friends, how much of that time is taken up with things that are ESSENTIAL?

_____ hours

VALUING TIME AS A COMMODITY YOU GIVE TO FAMILY & FRIENDS.

EXERCISE 4 – HOW MUCH DO YOU VALUE FAMILY & FRIENDS? HOW MUCH TIME WILL YOU GIVE TO THEM? (CONT'D)

QUESTION 7: How many hours are you left with when you take away the time spent on things that are not essential?   _____ hours

QUESTION 3: How does the revised amount of time feel?

_____

_____

_____

If you feel mainly positive, move forward with this amount of time.

If it doesn't feel mainly positive, go through questions 5, 6, 7 and 8 again until you do feel mainly positive.

Through answering the questions in this section, you've found out some information you wouldn't have if the questions had not been asked. On the following page we will summarize it to make it easier to digest...

WHAT IMPORTANT INFORMATION HAVE YOU FOUND OUT IN THIS SECTION THAT YOU EITHER DIDN'T KNOW OR DIDN'T REALLY THINK ABOUT, BEFORE YOU ANSWERED THE QUESTIONS?

The number of hours you are
contracted to work is: _____ hours

Your hourly rate for your contracted
hours is: _____

The number of hours you work in total,
including the free hours you give
to work is: _____ hours

Your hourly rate for all the hours you
work including free hours is: _____

The number of free hours you now feel
happy to work is: _____ hours

The number of hours you'd like to give
to yourself each day/week is: _____ hours

The number of hours you feel happy to
give to family and/or friends each
day/week is: _____ hours

PRIORITY:

a thing that is regarded as more important than others.

PRIORITISING YOUR TIME

 Prioritising workload time (including time you give for free)

 Prioritising YOU time.

Prioritising family & friends time.

Remember, the language I am using is all positive. None of this is about downgrading anything. It's about valuing and prioritising everything that is important to you. Then it's up to YOU what you do.

NOTHING is written in stone! All this book is showing you is what you are currently doing with your time and how you could use it in future. If you WANT MORE TIME, you'll apply what you're learning, if you don't, you won't!

In this section of the book, ONE EXERCISE FITS ALL. You will apply the same questions to each of your prioritising categories but I have provided you with the pages to carry out the prioritisation exercise for each category.

You can start with whichever one suits you but my advice would be to go for the one that feels easiest to do so that you reduce the level of difficulty.

If prioritising your workload currently feels like a TOUGH ASK, start with one of the others so that you familiarise yourself with the prioritisation process first.

Then, when you come to prioritising your workload you can focus on just that, rather than trying to understand the process too!

Prioritisation is the process of working out the level of importance or urgency of your tasks, activities, routines etc.

Regularly prioritising your workload will play a MAJOR role in REDUCING your stress levels because you will STOP seeing EVERYTHING as needing to be done YESTERDAY and START seeing the things that CAN WAIT until TOMORROW or do not need to be done at all!

Now, in my many coaching sessions with Teaching Assistants there is usually a good deal of resistance to prioritising workload. TAs start off by telling me it's not possible to prioritise tasks in school because so many things have equal importance. And my reply is ALWAYS the SAME:

'You already prioritise by choosing to do something FIRST. And then you do something SECOND, THIRD and so on!'

Your problem is, because you BELIEVE most of what you do is of EQUAL importance you're constantly JUGGLING tasks and playing a game of CATCH-UP, EVERY DAY!

And because, until now, you've not had any demarcation between work time and non work time, work takes up MOST of your time.

By prioritising tasks, you'll begin to see WHERE the tasks you're given, TRULY come, in their pecking order. You can also make others aware of this too, by asking THEM to rank, in order of priority, the tasks they give you.

Yes, you will ALWAYS have a list of things that need to be done. That is the nature of work – it never ends! BUT now that you've worked out, in the previous section, how many hours you're willing to give to your work, you will KNOW where your work STARTS and where it ENDS each day.

In this way you will have created DEMARCATION between WORK time, YOU time and FAMILY & FRIENDS time and work will no longer be this VAST thing occupying your physical time and your mental time, ALL OF THE TIME!

Now we will take each category of prioritisation i.e. WORKLOAD time, YOU time & FAMILY/FRIENDS time and ask you the questions you need to answer in order to prioritise each of them. I will begin with WORKLOAD TIME but you don't have to.

 **PRIORITISING WORKLOAD TIME**

1) MAKE A LIST OF ALL YOUR DAILY TASKS (DO NOT WORRY ABOUT PUTTING THEM IN ANY KIND OF ORDER, JUST LIST THEM)

IGNORE THE BOXES FOR NOW

PRIORITISING WORKLOAD TIME

2 GO BACK TO THE PREVIOUS INSTRUCTION AND RATE EACH TASK FROM 1-4 IN THE FOLLOWING WAY:

A TASK IS 1 IF IT IS URGENT AND IMPORTANT

A TASK IS 2 IF IT IS <u>NOT</u> URGENT AND IMPORTANT

A TASK IS 3 IF IT IS URGENT AND <u>NOT</u> IMPORTANT

A TASK IS 4 IF IT IS <u>NOT</u> URGENT AND <u>NOT</u> IMPORTANT
(FIND OUT MORE ABOUT THESE TASKS ON THE NEXT 4 PAGES)

Ask the opinion of colleagues, if it helps and DEFINITELY remember to ask the teacher(s) you work with to list the tasks they give you in order of priority. This will help them realise that you are not a task bin that they can dump everything in at once!

Keep giving out the message that you value the work you do for the children and the teachers you work with and this is why it's important that tasks are done in order of priority. And if you keep a pleasant smile on your face when you say it, so that no one detects any frustration from you, they'll be hard-put to argue with you!

PRIORITISING WORKLOAD TIME

TASKS THAT ARE URGENT AND IMPORTANT (1) ARE TASKS LIKE:

- dealing with emergencies and crises
- contacting parents and carers
- school meetings and training
- meeting important deadlines like assessments, marking (if you do it), reporting to your teacher
- other <u>immediately required</u> work specific to your role i.e. first-aid duty and tasks from a teacher listed as a top priority.

These are the kind of tasks that you do not have any real control over regarding their timeframe and requirements.

If you do not attend to these tasks as they arise, there could be serious consequences and you will experience much greater levels of stress, so, if it's an EMERGENCY, deal with it IMMEDIATELY, regardless of anything else you've been tasked to do.

Or, if it's a NON EMERGENCY but on the above list, GET IT DONE BEFORE ANYTHING ON YOUR OTHER LISTS unless it's time dependent i.e. has to be done at a specific time like a meeting later in the day etc.

PRIORITISING WORKLOAD TIME

TASKS THAT ARE NOT URGENT AND IMPORTANT (2) ARE TASKS LIKE:

- sourcing resources
- creating differentiated learning opportunities for children/groups you work with (if you are given any planning time for this)
- relationship building and pastoral care
- working on displays/class assemblies etc
- sorting non urgent issues children might have like lost clothing/property etc
- self-care

These are the kind of tasks you will find yourself doing on a daily basis. They're mainly what your job is all about. The more experienced you are, the quicker/efficient you will be at doing these tasks.

This could be an area where, if you find you've completed everything you <u>need</u> by the morning break and you're not on duty, that you actually sit down for 10 minutes with a cuppa! It's why I've added 'self-care' to this list because, if you find the time, take it! Think of it as part of VALUING TIME AS A COMMODITY YOU GIVE TO YOURSELF!

PRIORITISING WORKLOAD TIME

TASKS THAT ARE URGENT AND NOT IMPORTANT (3) ARE TASKS LIKE:

- above and beyond tasks like organising EVERY school disco, making costumes for EVERY play.
- attending too many meetings after school that are outside your contracted hours.
- general and regular interruptions where you've decided it's easier to 'do it yourself'.
- getting involved in other people's problems.

It can be really difficult to come away from the belief that you are all things to everyone, but it's THIS BELIEF that is SERIOUSLY taking up time that could be spent elsewhere.

So, rather than organise EVERY school disco, for instance, decide to organise one a year and allow others to have a go the rest of the time. In that way you free up more time for yourself or family and/or friends.

Being the person who sorts out other people's problems, eats into your time allowance. Give others some opportunity to become more self-sufficient so that they learn to solve their own problems.

PRIORITISING WORKLOAD TIME

TASKS THAT ARE NOT URGENT AND NOT IMPORTANT (4) ARE TASKS LIKE:

- spending too much time thinking about one particular thing/issue.
- getting involved with the 'rumour mill'.
- constantly tweaking something to make it even better.
- mindlessly scrolling through social media.
- beautifying the class environment.

When you look around a classroom, you will always find something to do but if it comes under the label of 'beautifying' PLEASE RESIST!

Beautifying includes stuff like replacing everything when only some of it is damaged, getting involved in tidying the classroom, trying to get a stain out of the carpet, repairing furniture etc.

And there is always someone with something to moan about. Sympathise by all means but don't get involved! Speculation and gossip, whilst you may enjoy them, are a dreadful waste of your precious time. When you decide not to entertain them, you immediately feel lighter and RELEASE MORE TIME!

PRIORITISING WORKLOAD TIME

NOW THAT YOU HAVE SOME GRASP OF THE SYSTEM, GIVE IT A GO YOURSELF!

The next few pages will enable you to take your daily tasks that you've rated 1-4 categories and choose a couple from each category to work on.

And, to be clear, this system is not mine. It's known as the Eisenhower Principle and is used specifically for time management. Of all the systems I've tried, this one has given me the most success. If you want to find out more about it just do an internet search for 'Eisenhower Principle'.

PRIORITISING WORKLOAD TIME

MY CATEGORY 1 (URGENT AND IMPORTANT) TASKS ARE:

_____ _____

_____ _____

_____ _____

_____ _____

_____ _____

_____ _____

These tasks ALWAYS either take PRIORITY over ANYTHING else that is going on OR must be completed within a certain time to AVOID SERIOUS CONSEQUENCES.

PRIORITISING WORKLOAD TIME

MY CATEGORY 2 (NOT URGENT AND IMPORTANT) TASKS ARE:

_____ ☐   _____ ☐

_____ ☐   _____ ☐

_____ ☐   _____ ☐

_____ ☐   _____ ☐

_____ ☐   _____ ☐

_____ ☐   _____ ☐

_____ ☐   _____ ☐

_____ ☐   _____ ☐

_____ ☐   _____ ☐

These are the tasks you do on a daily basis and whilst it may not be possible to remove or reduce them, it is possible for you to prioritise them on a scale of 1-3, with 1 being a range of tasks that must be done first and 3 being a range of tasks that can be done last.

Use the boxes to prioritse them 1-3

PRIORITISING WORKLOAD TIME

MY CATEGORY 3 (URGENT AND NOT IMPORTANT) TASKS ARE:

These are the tasks you do because you believe you can be all things to everyone, or the go to person to sort out other people's problems.

Choose one or two of these to reduce or stop doing altogether, whichever feels most comfortable to you.

Tick a box for whichever tasks you are going to work on or use a number system i.e. the lowest number being the task you're currently working on with higher numbers being tasks you've already worked on.

PRIORITISING WORKLOAD TIME

MY CATEGORY 4 (NOT URGENT AND NOT IMPORTANT) TASKS ARE:

_____ ☐	_____ ☐
_____ ☐	_____ ☐
_____ ☐	_____ ☐
_____ ☐	_____ ☐
_____ ☐	_____ ☐
_____ ☐	_____ ☐
_____ ☐	_____ ☐
_____ ☐	_____ ☐

These are the tasks we all find ourselves doing because they feel good like replacing all the labels on a set of drawers because one of them is looking tatty etc. Or they're tasks we engage in mindlessly because we haven't worked out a better way to use our time.

Tick a box for whichever tasks you are going to stop doing or use a number system i.e. the lowest number being the task you're currently working on with higher numbers being tasks you've already worked on.

Now we will

Repeat the

process

as we

focus on

you

time!

PRIORITISING YOU TIME

1) 1 MAKE A LIST OF ALL YOUR DAILY TASKS YOU DO AT HOME INCLUDING EVERYTHING YOU DO FOR OTHERS (DO NOT WORRY ABOUT PUTTING THEM IN ANY KIND OF ORDER, JUST LIST THEM)

IGNORE THE BOXES FOR NOW

PRIORITISING YOU TIME

2 GO BACK TO THE PREVIOUS INSTRUCTION AND RATE EACH TASK FROM 1-4 IN THE FOLLOWING WAY:

A TASK IS 1 IF IT IS URGENT AND IMPORTANT

A TASK IS 2 IF IT IS <u>NOT</u> URGENT AND IMPORTANT

A TASK IS 3 IF IT IS URGENT AND <u>NOT</u> IMPORTANT

A TASK IS 4 IF IT IS <u>NOT</u> URGENT AND <u>NOT</u> IMPORTANT
(FIND OUT MORE ABOUT THESE TASKS ON THE NEXT 4 PAGES)

Ask the opinion of relatives or friends, if it helps and get into the habit of asking anyone at home who regularly wants your help to rank it by how important it is to them. This will help them realise that you are not a task bin that they can dump everything in at once!

This is an opportunity for you to start giving out the message that whilst you are always willing to help where necessary, you are no longer willing to foster 'learned helplessness' in your loved ones. Give them opportunities to learn and grow by being more independent.

PRIORITISING YOU TIME

TASKS THAT ARE URGENT AND IMPORTANT (1) ARE TASKS LIKE:

- dealing with emergencies and crises
- contacting companies to renew insurance or pay utility bills etc.
- your children's school open evenings.
- GP and hospital appointments etc.
- other <u>immediately required</u> work specific to your family circumstances

These are the kind of tasks that you do not have any real control over regarding their timeframe and requirements.

If you do not attend to these tasks as they arise, there could be serious consequences and you will experience much greater levels of stress, so, if it's an EMERGENCY, deal with it IMMEDIATELY, regardless of anything else you've been tasked to do.

Or, if it's a NON EMERGENCY but on the above list, GET IT DONE BEFORE ANYTHING ON YOUR OTHER LISTS unless it's time dependent i.e. has to be done at a specific time like a doctor/dental appointment.

PRIORITISING YOU TIME

TASKS THAT ARE NOT URGENT AND IMPORTANT (2) ARE TASKS LIKE:

- shopping
- cooking
- cleaning
- laundry
- helping children with homework
- taking children to visit friends etc
- spending time with your partner
- chatting to relatives and/or friends
- taking the dog for a walk
- gardening
- anything else related to family life you do regularly

These are the kind of tasks you will find yourself doing on a daily basis because they are what family life is all about.

Whilst many of these tasks are of course necessary, start thinking about whether YOU always need to do ALL of them. Try to reduce any perfectionism by letting others have a go! In this way you can free up some well deserved YOU time!

PRIORITISING YOU TIME

TASKS THAT ARE URGENT AND NOT IMPORTANT (3) ARE TASKS LIKE:

- above and beyond tasks like being the entertainer for ALL of your children's birthday parties.
- being too rigid with how often and how perfectly you do the housework/cooking etc.
- general and regular interruptions where you've decided it's easier to 'do it yourself'.
- getting involved in other people's problems.

It can be really difficult to come away from the 'perfect housewife' scenario but trying to fulfil this unrealistic expectation just reduces the time you have either for yourself of family/friends.

So, rather than cook healthy and tasty meals EVERY evening, for instance, have a night or 2 off where you have a convenience meal, take-away or let someone else cook!

And being the person who sorts out other people's problems eats into your time allowance. Give others some opportunity to become more self-sufficient so that they learn to solve their own problems.

PRIORITISING YOU TIME

TASKS THAT ARE NOT URGENT AND NOT IMPORTANT (4) ARE TASKS LIKE:

- spending too much time thinking about one particular thing/issue.
- watching the news and worrying about the future.
- constantly tweaking something to make it even better.
- mindlessly scrolling through social media
- arriving at appointments way too early

Because we have brains that can analyse, we sometimes find ourselves in a state of 'analysis paralysis' where we are spending too much time thinking about an issue rather than dealing with it.

Likewise, we can spend a good deal of time worrying about future events that may never happen. A good remedy for this is to severly limit the amount of news you watch!

And, when you catch yourself scrolling mindlessly through social media, STOP! There are so many things you coud be doing for YOURSELF that are BETTER than that!

PRIORITISING YOU TIME

NOW THAT YOU HAVE SOME GRASP OF THE SYSTEM, GIVE IT A GO YOURSELF!

The next few pages will enable you to take your daily tasks that you've rated 1-4 categories and choose a couple from each category to work on.

PRIORITISING YOU TIME

MY CATEGORY 1 (URGENT AND IMPORTANT) TASKS ARE:

_____   _____

_____   _____

_____   _____

_____   _____

_____   _____

_____   _____

_____   _____

These tasks ALWAYS either take PRIORITY over ANYTHING else that is going on OR must be completed within a certain time to AVOID SERIOUS CONSEQUENCES.

PRIORITISING YOU TIME

MY CATEGORY 2 (NOT URGENT AND IMPORTANT) TASKS ARE:

These are the tasks you do on a daily basis and whilst it may not be possible to remove or reduce them, it is possible for you to prioritise them on a scale of 1-3, with 1 being a range of tasks that must be done first and 3 being a range of tasks that can be done last.

Use the boxes to prioritse them 1-3

PRIORITISING YOU TIME

MY CATEGORY 3 (URGENT AND NOT IMPORTANT) TASKS ARE:

These are the tasks you do because you believe you can be all things to everyone, or the go to person to sort out other people's problems.

Choose one or two of these to reduce or stop doing altogether, whichever feels most comfortable to you.

Tick a box for whichever tasks you are going to work on or use a number system i.e. the lowest number being the task you're currently working on with higher numbers being tasks you've already worked on.

PRIORITISING YOU TIME

MY CATEGORY 4 (NOT URGENT AND NOT IMPORTANT) TASKS
ARE:

These are the tasks we all find ourselves doing because they feel good like washing all the paintwork just because one bit of it needs attention etc. Or they're tasks we engage in mindlessly because we haven't worked out a better way to use our time.

Tick a box for whichever tasks you are going to stop doing or use a number system i.e. the lowest number being the task you're currently working on with higher numbers being tasks you've already worked on.

PRIORITISING YOU TIME

NOW CREATE A LIST OF ALL THE THINGS YOU LIKE TO DO FOR YOURSELF:

_____ ☐   _____ ☐

_____ ☐   _____ ☐

_____ ☐   _____ ☐

_____ ☐   _____ ☐

_____ ☐   _____ ☐

_____ ☐   _____ ☐

_____ ☐   _____ ☐

_____ ☐   _____ ☐

Use the above slots to make a list of all the things you like to do.

Then use a number system to indicate which of the above you want to start weaving in to your day, with 1 being top priority and a lower number being less of a priority.

Having worked out which of your general home and family tasks are neither urgent or important, you should now have some time to include some things just for you!

Now we will repeat the process as we focus on family/friends time!

PRIORITISING FAMILY/FRIENDS TIME

1) 1 MAKE A LIST OF ALL THE THINGS YOU CURRENTLY DO JUST FOR FAMILY AND/OR FRIENDS (DO NOT WORRY ABOUT PUTTING THEM IN ANY KIND OF ORDER, JUST LIST THEM)

IGNORE THE BOXES FOR NOW

PRIORITISING FAMILY/FRIENDS TIME

2 GO BACK TO THE PREVIOUS INSTRUCTION AND RATE EACH TASK FROM 1-4 IN THE FOLLOWING WAY:

A TASK IS 1 IF IT IS URGENT AND IMPORTANT

A TASK IS 2 IF IT IS <u>NOT</u> URGENT AND IMPORTANT

A TASK IS 3 IF IT IS URGENT AND <u>NOT</u> IMPORTANT

A TASK IS 4 IF IT IS <u>NOT</u> URGENT AND <u>NOT</u> IMPORTANT
(FIND OUT MORE ABOUT THESE TASKS ON THE NEXT 4 PAGES)

Ask the opinion of relatives or friends, if it helps and get into the habit of asking anyone at home who regularly wants your help to rank it by how important it is to them. This will help them realise that you are not a task bin that they can dump everything in at once!

This is an opportunity for you to start giving out the message that whilst you are always willing to help where necessary, you are no longer willing to foster 'learned helplessness' in your loved ones. Give them opportunities to learn and grow by being more independent.

PRIORITISING FAMILY/FRIENDS TIME

TASKS THAT ARE URGENT AND IMPORTANT (1) ARE TASKS LIKE:

- dealing with emergencies and crises
- supporting family/friends when they have a major issue going on
- picking up relatives/friends children from school or babysitting etc
- taking elderly relatives for appointments etc
- other <u>immediately required</u> work specific to your family/friends circumstances

These are the kind of tasks that you do not have any real control over regarding their timeframe and requirements.

If you do not attend to these tasks as they arise, there could be serious consequences and you will experience much greater levels of stress, so, if it's an EMERGENCY, deal with it IMMEDIATELY, regardless of anything else you've been tasked to do.

Or, if it's a NON EMERGENCY but on the above list, GET IT DONE BEFORE ANYTHING ON YOUR OTHER LISTS unless it's time dependent i.e. has to be done at a specific time like a doctor/dental appointment.

PRIORITISING FAMILY/FRIENDS TIME

TASKS THAT ARE NOT URGENT AND IMPORTANT (2) ARE TASKS LIKE:

- taking older relatives for routine appointments.
- regular babysitting you've agreed to do.
- visiting relatives.
- going out with friends.
- helping children with homework.
- taking children to visit friends etc.
- spending time with your partner.
- chatting to relatives and/or friends.
- attending celebrations - birthdays etc.
- shopping for elderly relatives.
- anything else related to family life you do regularly.

These are the kind of tasks you will find yourself doing on a daily/weekly basis because they are what family life and having friends is all about.

Whilst many of these tasks are of course necessary, start thinking about whether YOU always need to do ALL of them. Try to reduce any perfectionism by letting others have a go! In this way you can free up some well deserved YOU time!

PRIORITISING FAMILY/FRIENDS TIME

TASKS THAT ARE URGENT AND NOT IMPORTANT (3) ARE TASKS LIKE:

- above and beyond tasks like making a cake every time a relative or friend has a birthday.
- feeling like you must visit certain relatives on a weekly basis.
- general and regular interruptions where you've decided it's easier to 'do it yourself'.
- getting too involved in relatives or friends ongoing issues.

It can be really difficult to come away from the 'perfect daughter/friend' scenario but trying to fulfil this unrealistic expectation just reduces the time you have either for other things.

So, rather than visit your parents, say, every week, try doing a couple of Zoom calls during a week when you've decided not to visit.

And rather than YOU being your friends' 'go to' person EVERY TIME they have an issue, help them to help themselves from time to time or get other friends to step up.

PRIORITISING FAMILY/FRIENDS TIME

TASKS THAT ARE NOT URGENT AND NOT IMPORTANT (4) ARE TASKS LIKE:

- spending too much time thinking about one particular thing/issue.
- worrying about elderly relatives.
- constantly checking in on relatives/friends via social media.
- chatting to family/friends on the phone too often.
- getting too involved in other people's arguments.

Because we have brains that can analyse, we sometimes find ourselves in a state of 'analysis paralysis' where we are spending too much time thinking about an issue rather than dealing with it.

Likewise, we can spend a good deal of time worrying elderly relatives. A good remedy for this is to ask yourself if someone is currently safe and okay, if not completely well. Most of the time the answer will be 'yes'.

And, when you catch yourself about to phone a relative or friend just because you're having an idle moment, ask yourself if there is something you could do, instead, that is SOLELY for YOU.

PRIORITISING FAMILY/FRIENDS TIME

NOW THAT YOU HAVE SOME GRASP OF THE SYSTEM, GIVE IT A GO YOURSELF!

The next few pages will enable you to take your daily tasks that you've rated 1-4 categories and choose a couple from each category to work on.

PRIORITISING FAMILY/FRIENDS TIME

MY CATEGORY 1 (URGENT AND IMPORTANT) TASKS ARE:

_____   _____

_____   _____

_____   _____

_____   _____

_____   _____

_____   _____

These tasks ALWAYS either take PRIORITY over ANYTHING else that is going on OR must be completed within a certain time to AVOID SERIOUS CONSEQUENCES.

PRIORITISING FAMILY/FRIENDS TIME

MY CATEGORY 2 (NOT URGENT AND IMPORTANT) TASKS ARE:

_____ ☐   _____ ☐

_____ ☐   _____ ☐

_____ ☐   _____ ☐

_____ ☐   _____ ☐

_____ ☐   _____ ☐

_____ ☐   _____ ☐

_____ ☐   _____ ☐

_____ ☐   _____ ☐

_____ ☐   _____ ☐

_____ ☐   _____ ☐

These are the tasks you do on a daily basis and whilst it may not be possible to remove or reduce them, it is possible for you to prioritise them on a scale of 1-3, with 1 being a range of tasks that must be done first and 3 being a range of tasks that can be done last.

Use the boxes to prioritse them 1-3

PRIORITISING FAMILY/FRIENDS TIME

MY CATEGORY 3 (URGENT AND NOT IMPORTANT) TASKS ARE:

These are the tasks you do because you believe you can be all things to everyone, or the go to person to sort out other people's problems.

Choose one or two of these to reduce or stop doing altogether, whichever feels most comfortable to you.

Tick a box for whichever tasks you are going to work on or use a number system i.e. the lowest number being the task you're currently working on with higher numbers being tasks you've already worked on.

PRIORITISING FAMILY/FRIENDS TIME

MY CATEGORY 4 (NOT URGENT AND NOT IMPORTANT) TASKS ARE:

_____ ☐   _____ ☐

_____ ☐   _____ ☐

_____ ☐   _____ ☐

_____ ☐   _____ ☐

_____ ☐   _____ ☐

_____ ☐   _____ ☐

_____ ☐   _____ ☐

_____ ☐   _____ ☐

_____ ☐   _____ ☐

These are the tasks we all find ourselves doing because they feel good like trying to find the very best apples for the relative you're shopping for etc. Or they're tasks we engage in mindlessly because we haven't worked out a better way to use our time.

Tick a box for whichever tasks you are going to stop doing or use a number system i.e. the lowest number being the task you're currently working on with higher numbers being tasks you've already worked on.

JOURNALING:

A personal record of occurrences, experiences, and reflections kept on a regular basis.

REFLECTING ON YOUR TIME

You now have 30 days of journaling pages that will help you work out which of the VALUING and PRIORITISING exercises is working well for you.

This will give you the opportunity to BRING YOURSELF fully in alignment with the exercises you have already completed because it doesn't matter how efficiently we plan, if something doesn't FEEL right to us, we're unlikely to do it.

So, for the next 30 days you have the chance to plan out your day including your PAID WORK time, the time you will give for FREE to your workplace, YOU time and FAMILY/FRIENDS time and then at the end of each day you can write about how your day went including what went well for you.

I will also ask you to reflect on the different aspects of your day that you ENJOYED to help you work out how to create MORE ENJOYMENT.

The trouble for most hardworking people is that, from a young age, we are brain-washed into thinking that life IS HARD, in the belief that this will help us cope. And, of course, life can be hard but there are many parts of your day that could be more enjoyable, if you put your mind to figuring out how...

TIME SPENT ON QUIET REFLECTION IS TIME WELL SPENT!

DAY 1

DATE: _____

PLANNING AND JOURNALING!

In addition to my general TA duties today, I would like to complete or reduce these tasks (I've given you room to write 6 but please do not feel 6 is the goal unless you want it to be!):

_____   _____

_____   _____

_____   _____

I am giving my school _____ minutes/hours of FREE TIME today so that I complete or reduce these tasks (6 doesn't have to be the goal!):

_____   _____

_____   _____

_____   _____

I am giving myself _____ minutes/hours of ME TIME today to give myself time to relax/do something I enjoy (again, 6 does not have to be the goal):

_____   _____

_____   _____

_____   _____

ME TIME will be at   _____ _____ _____
these times: _____ _____ _____

The tasks I am doing for FAMILY/FRIENDS today are (I have given you space for 10 but you can do less!)

_____   _____

_____   _____

_____   _____

_____   _____

_____   _____

Write down 3 things that went well today:

_____

_____

_____

Write down 3 things I enjoyed today:

_____

_____

_____

What have I learned from today that will help me enjoy tomorrow?:

_____

_____

_____

DAY 2

PLANNING AND JOURNALING!

In addition to my general TA duties today, I would like to complete or reduce these tasks (I've given you room to write 6 but please do not feel 6 is the goal unless you want it to be!):

_____ _____

_____ _____

_____ _____

I am giving my school _____ minutes/hours of FREE TIME today so that I complete or reduce these tasks (again, 6 does not have to be the goal!):

_____ _____

_____ _____

_____ _____

I am giving myself _____ minutes/hours of ME TIME today to give myself time to relax/do something I enjoy (again, 6 does not have to be the goal):

_____ _____

_____ _____

_____ _____

ME TIME will be at these times: _____ _____ _____

_____ _____ _____

The tasks I am doing for FAMILY/FRIENDS today are (I have given you space for 10 but you can do less!)

_____   _____

_____   _____

_____   _____

_____   _____

_____   _____

Write down 3 things that went well today:

_____

_____

_____

Write down 3 things I enjoyed today:

_____

_____

_____

What have I learned from today that will help me enjoy tomorrow?:

_____

_____

_____

DAY 3

DATE: _____

PLANNING AND JOURNALING!

In addition to my general TA duties today, I would like to complete or reduce these tasks (I've given you room to write 6 but please do not feel 6 is the goal unless you want it to be!):

_____   _____

_____   _____

_____   _____

I am giving my school _____ minutes/hours of FREE TIME today so that I complete or reduce these tasks (again, 6 does not have to be the goal!):

_____   _____

_____   _____

_____   _____

I am giving myself _____ minutes/hours of ME TIME today to give myself time to relax/do something I enjoy (again, 6 does not have to be the goal):

_____   _____

_____   _____

_____   _____

ME TIME will be at these times: _____ _____ _____

_____ _____ _____

The tasks I am doing for FAMILY/FRIENDS today are (I have given you space for 10 but you can do less!)

_____   _____

_____   _____

_____   _____

_____   _____

_____   _____

Write down 3 things that went well today:

_____

_____

_____

Write down 3 things I enjoyed today:

_____

_____

_____

What have I learned from today that will help me enjoy tomorrow?:

_____

_____

_____

DAY 4

PLANNING AND JOURNALING!

In addition to my general TA duties today, I would like to complete or reduce these tasks (I've given you room to write 6 but please do not feel 6 is the goal unless you want it to be!):

_____   _____

_____   _____

_____   _____

I am giving my school _____ minutes/hours of FREE TIME today so that I complete or reduce these tasks (again, 6 does not have to be the goal!):

_____   _____

_____   _____

_____   _____

I am giving myself _____ minutes/hours of ME TIME today to give myself time to relax/do something I enjoy (again, 6 does not have to be the goal):

_____   _____

_____   _____

_____   _____

ME TIME will be at   _____ _____ _____
these times: _____ _____ _____

The tasks I am doing for FAMILY/FRIENDS today are (I have given you space for 10 but you can do less!)

_____   _____

_____   _____

_____   _____

_____   _____

_____   _____

Write down 3 things that went well today:

_____

_____

_____

Write down 3 things I enjoyed today:

_____

_____

_____

What have I learned from today that will help me enjoy tomorrow?:

_____

_____

_____

DAY 5

PLANNING AND JOURNALING!

In addition to my general TA duties today, I would like to complete or reduce these tasks (I've given you room to write 6 but please do not feel 6 is the goal unless you want it to be!):

_____   _____

_____   _____

_____   _____

I am giving my school _____ minutes/hours of FREE TIME today so that I complete or reduce these tasks (again, 6 does not have to be the goal!):

_____   _____

_____   _____

_____   _____

I am giving myself _____ minutes/hours of ME TIME today to give myself time to relax/do something I enjoy (again, 6 does not have to be the goal):

_____   _____

_____   _____

_____   _____

ME TIME will be at   _____ _____ _____
these times: _____ _____ _____

The tasks I am doing for FAMILY/FRIENDS today are (I have given you space for 10 but you can do less!)

_____   _____

_____   _____

_____   _____

_____   _____

_____   _____

Write down 3 things that went well today:

_____

_____

_____

Write down 3 things I enjoyed today:

_____

_____

_____

What have I learned from today that will help me enjoy tomorrow?:

_____

_____

_____

DAY 6

PLANNING AND JOURNALING!

In addition to my general TA duties today, I would like to complete or reduce these tasks (I've given you room to write 6 but please do not feel 6 is the goal unless you want it to be!):

_____   _____

_____   _____

_____   _____

I am giving my school _____ minutes/hours of FREE TIME today so that I complete or reduce these tasks (again, 6 does not have to be the goal!):

_____   _____

_____   _____

_____   _____

I am giving myself _____ minutes/hours of ME TIME today to give myself time to relax/do something I enjoy (again, 6 does not have to be the goal):

_____   _____

_____   _____

_____   _____

ME TIME will be at   _____ _____ _____
these times: _____ _____ _____

The tasks I am doing for **FAMILY/FRIENDS** today are (I have given you space for 10 but you can do less!)

_____ _____

_____ _____

_____ _____

_____ _____

_____ _____

Write down 3 things that went well today:

_____

_____

_____

Write down 3 things I enjoyed today:

_____

_____

_____

What have I learned from today that will help me enjoy tomorrow?:

_____

_____

_____

_____

DAY 7

DATE: _____

PLANNING AND JOURNALING!

In addition to my general TA duties today, I would like to complete or reduce these tasks (I've given you room to write 6 but please do not feel 6 is the goal unless you want it to be!):

_____   _____

_____   _____

_____   _____

I am giving my school _____ minutes/hours of FREE TIME today so that I complete or reduce these tasks (again, 6 does not have to be the goal!):

_____   _____

_____   _____

_____   _____

I am giving myself _____ minutes/hours of ME TIME today to give myself time to relax/do something I enjoy (again, 6 does not have to be the goal):

_____   _____

_____   _____

_____   _____

ME TIME will be at these times: _____ _____ _____

_____ _____ _____

The tasks I am doing for **FAMILY/FRIENDS** today are (I have given you space for 10 but you can do less!)

_____   _____

_____   _____

_____   _____

_____   _____

_____   _____

Write down 3 things that went well today:

_____

_____

_____

Write down 3 things I enjoyed today:

_____

_____

_____

What have I learned from today that will help me enjoy tomorrow?:

_____

_____

_____

DATE: _____

PLANNING AND JOURNALING!

In addition to my general TA duties today, I would like to complete or reduce these tasks (I've given you room to write 6 but please do not feel 6 is the goal unless you want it to be!):

_____   _____

_____   _____

_____   _____

I am giving my school _____ minutes/hours of FREE TIME today so that I complete or reduce these tasks (again, 6 does not have to be the goal!):

_____   _____

_____   _____

_____   _____

I am giving myself _____ minutes/hours of ME TIME today to give myself time to relax/do something I enjoy (again, 6 does not have to be the goal):

_____   _____

_____   _____

_____   _____

ME TIME will be at   _____ _____ _____
these times: _____ _____ _____

The tasks I am doing for FAMILY/FRIENDS today are (I have given you space for 10 but you can do less!)

_____   _____

_____   _____

_____   _____

_____   _____

_____   _____

Write down 3 things that went well today:

_____

_____

_____

Write down 3 things I enjoyed today:

_____

_____

_____

What have I learned from today that will help me enjoy tomorrow?:

_____

_____

_____

DATE: _____

PLANNING AND JOURNALING!

In addition to my general TA duties today, I would like to complete or reduce these tasks (I've given you room to write 6 but please do not feel 6 is the goal unless you want it to be!):

_____   _____

_____   _____

_____   _____

I am giving my school _____ minutes/hours of FREE TIME today so that I complete or reduce these tasks (again, 6 does not have to be the goal!):

_____   _____

_____   _____

_____   _____

I am giving myself _____ minutes/hours of ME TIME today to give myself time to relax/do something I enjoy (again, 6 does not have to be the goal):

_____   _____

_____   _____

_____   _____

ME TIME will be at these times: _____ _____ _____

_____ _____ _____

The tasks I am doing for FAMILY/FRIENDS today are (I have given you space for 10 but you can do less!)

_____   _____

_____   _____

_____   _____

_____   _____

_____   _____

Write down 3 things that went well today:

_____

_____

_____

Write down 3 things I enjoyed today:

_____

_____

_____

What have I learned from today that will help me enjoy tomorrow?:

_____

_____

_____

DATE: _____

PLANNING AND JOURNALING!

In addition to my general TA duties today, I would like to complete or reduce these tasks (I've given you room to write 6 but please do not feel 6 is the goal unless you want it to be!):

_____   _____

_____   _____

_____   _____

I am giving my school _____ minutes/hours of FREE TIME today so that I complete or reduce these tasks (again, 6 does not have to be the goal!):

_____   _____

_____   _____

_____   _____

I am giving myself _____ minutes/hours of ME TIME today to give myself time to relax/do something I enjoy (again, 6 does not have to be the goal):

_____   _____

_____   _____

_____   _____

ME TIME will be at these times: _____ _____ _____

_____ _____ _____

The tasks I am doing for FAMILY/FRIENDS today are (I have given you space for 10 but you can do less!)

_____   _____

_____   _____

_____   _____

_____   _____

_____   _____

Write down 3 things that went well today:

_____

_____

_____

Write down 3 things I enjoyed today:

_____

_____

_____

What have I learned from today that will help me enjoy tomorrow?:

_____

_____

_____

DATE: _____

PLANNING AND JOURNALING!

In addition to my general TA duties today, I would like to complete or reduce these tasks (I've given you room to write 6 but please do not feel 6 is the goal unless you want it to be!):

_____   _____

_____   _____

_____   _____

I am giving my school _____ minutes/hours of FREE TIME today so that I complete or reduce these tasks (again, 6 does not have to be the goal!):

_____   _____

_____   _____

_____   _____

I am giving myself _____ minutes/hours of ME TIME today to give myself time to relax/do something I enjoy (again, 6 does not have to be the goal):

_____   _____

_____   _____

_____   _____

ME TIME will be at these times: _____ _____ _____

_____ _____ _____

The tasks I am doing for FAMILY/FRIENDS today are (I have given you space for 10 but you can do less!)

_____   _____

_____   _____

_____   _____

_____   _____

_____   _____

Write down 3 things that went well today:

_____

_____

_____

Write down 3 things I enjoyed today:

_____

_____

_____

What have I learned from today that will help me enjoy tomorrow?:

_____

_____

_____

DAY 12

PLANNING AND JOURNALING!

In addition to my general TA duties today, I would like to complete or reduce these tasks (I've given you room to write 6 but please do not feel 6 is the goal unless you want it to be!):

_____   _____

_____   _____

_____   _____

I am giving my school _____ minutes/hours of FREE TIME today so that I complete or reduce these tasks (again, 6 does not have to be the goal!):

_____   _____

_____   _____

_____   _____

I am giving myself _____ minutes/hours of ME TIME today to give myself time to relax/do something I enjoy (again, 6 does not have to be the goal):

_____   _____

_____   _____

_____   _____

ME TIME will be at these times: _____ _____ _____

_____ _____ _____

The tasks I am doing for FAMILY/FRIENDS today are (I have given you space for 10 but you can do less!)

_____   _____

_____   _____

_____   _____

_____   _____

_____   _____

Write down 3 things that went well today:

_____

_____

_____

Write down 3 things I enjoyed today:

_____

_____

_____

What have I learned from today that will help me enjoy tomorrow?:

_____

_____

_____

DAY 13

PLANNING AND JOURNALING!

In addition to my general TA duties today, I would like to complete or reduce these tasks (I've given you room to write 6 but please do not feel 6 is the goal unless you want it to be!):

_____   _____

_____   _____

_____   _____

I am giving my school _____ minutes/hours of FREE TIME today so that I complete or reduce these tasks (again, 6 does not have to be the goal!):

_____   _____

_____   _____

_____   _____

I am giving myself _____ minutes/hours of ME TIME today to give myself time to relax/do something I enjoy (again, 6 does not have to be the goal):

_____   _____

_____   _____

_____   _____

ME TIME will be at these times: _____ _____ _____

_____ _____ _____

The tasks I am doing for FAMILY/FRIENDS today are (I have given you space for 10 but you can do less!)

_____   _____

_____   _____

_____   _____

_____   _____

_____   _____

Write down 3 things that went well today:

_____

_____

_____

Write down 3 things I enjoyed today:

_____

_____

_____

What have I learned from today that will help me enjoy tomorrow?:

_____

_____

_____

DAY 14

PLANNING AND JOURNALING!

In addition to my general TA duties today, I would like to complete or reduce these tasks (I've given you room to write 6 but please do not feel 6 is the goal unless you want it to be!):

_____   _____

_____   _____

_____   _____

I am giving my school _____ minutes/hours of FREE TIME today so that I complete or reduce these tasks (again, 6 does not have to be the goal!):

_____   _____

_____   _____

_____   _____

I am giving myself _____ minutes/hours of ME TIME today to give myself time to relax/do something I enjoy (again, 6 does not have to be the goal):

_____   _____

_____   _____

_____   _____

ME TIME will be at   _____ _____ _____
these times: _____ _____ _____

The tasks I am doing for FAMILY/FRIENDS today are (I have given you space for 10 but you can do less!)

_____   _____

_____   _____

_____   _____

_____   _____

_____   _____

Write down 3 things that went well today:

_____

_____

_____

Write down 3 things I enjoyed today:

_____

_____

_____

What have I learned from today that will help me enjoy tomorrow?:

_____

_____

_____

DAY 15

DATE: _____

PLANNING AND JOURNALING!

In addition to my general TA duties today, I would like to complete or reduce these tasks (I've given you room to write 6 but please do not feel 6 is the goal unless you want it to be!):

_____   _____

_____   _____

_____   _____

I am giving my school _____ minutes/hours of FREE TIME today so that I complete or reduce these tasks (again, 6 does not have to be the goal!):

_____   _____

_____   _____

_____   _____

I am giving myself _____ minutes/hours of ME TIME today to give myself time to relax/do something I enjoy (again, 6 does not have to be the goal):

_____   _____

_____   _____

_____   _____

ME TIME will be at these times: _____ _____ _____

_____ _____ _____

The tasks I am doing for FAMILY/FRIENDS today are (I have given you space for 10 but you can do less!)

_____   _____

_____   _____

_____   _____

_____   _____

_____   _____

Write down 3 things that went well today:

_____

_____

_____

Write down 3 things I enjoyed today:

_____

_____

_____

What have I learned from today that will help me enjoy tomorrow?:

_____

_____

_____

DAY 16

PLANNING AND JOURNALING!

In addition to my general TA duties today, I would like to complete or reduce these tasks (I've given you room to write 6 but please do not feel 6 is the goal unless you want it to be!):

_____   _____

_____   _____

_____   _____

I am giving my school _____ minutes/hours of FREE TIME today so that I complete or reduce these tasks (again, 6 does not have to be the goal!):

_____   _____

_____   _____

_____   _____

I am giving myself _____ minutes/hours of ME TIME today to give myself time to relax/do something I enjoy (again, 6 does not have to be the goal):

_____   _____

_____   _____

_____   _____

ME TIME will be at these times: _____ _____ _____

_____ _____ _____

The tasks I am doing for FAMILY/FRIENDS today are (I have given you space for 10 but you can do less!)

_____   _____

_____   _____

_____   _____

_____   _____

_____   _____

Write down 3 things that went well today:

_____

_____

_____

Write down 3 things I enjoyed today:

_____

_____

_____

What have I learned from today that will help me enjoy tomorrow?:

_____

_____

_____

_____

DAY 17

PLANNING AND JOURNALING!

In addition to my general TA duties today, I would like to complete or reduce these tasks (I've given you room to write 6 but please do not feel 6 is the goal unless you want it to be!):

_____   _____

_____   _____

_____   _____

I am giving my school _____ minutes/hours of FREE TIME today so that I complete or reduce these tasks (again, 6 does not have to be the goal!):

_____   _____

_____   _____

_____   _____

I am giving myself _____ minutes/hours of ME TIME today to give myself time to relax/do something I enjoy (again, 6 does not have to be the goal):

_____   _____

_____   _____

_____   _____

ME TIME will be at   _____ _____ _____
these times: _____ _____ _____

The tasks I am doing for FAMILY/FRIENDS today are (I have given you space for 10 but you can do less!)

_____   _____

_____   _____

_____   _____

_____   _____

_____   _____

Write down 3 things that went well today:

_____

_____

_____

Write down 3 things I enjoyed today:

_____

_____

_____

What have I learned from today that will help me enjoy tomorrow?:

_____

_____

_____

DATE: _____

PLANNING AND JOURNALING!

In addition to my general TA duties today, I would like to complete or reduce these tasks (I've given you room to write 6 but please do not feel 6 is the goal unless you want it to be!):

_____   _____

_____   _____

_____   _____

I am giving my school _____ minutes/hours of FREE TIME today so that I complete or reduce these tasks (again, 6 does not have to be the goal!):

_____   _____

_____   _____

_____   _____

I am giving myself _____ minutes/hours of ME TIME today to give myself time to relax/do something I enjoy (again, 6 does not have to be the goal):

_____   _____

_____   _____

_____   _____

ME TIME will be at these times: _____ _____ _____

_____ _____ _____

The tasks I am doing for FAMILY/FRIENDS today are (I have given you space for 10 but you can do less!)

_____   _____

_____   _____

_____   _____

_____   _____

_____   _____

Write down 3 things that went well today:

_____

_____

_____

Write down 3 things I enjoyed today:

_____

_____

_____

What have I learned from today that will help me enjoy tomorrow?:

_____

_____

_____

DATE: _____

PLANNING AND JOURNALING!

In addition to my general TA duties today, I would like to complete or reduce these tasks (I've given you room to write 6 but please do not feel 6 is the goal unless you want it to be!):

_____   _____

_____   _____

_____   _____

I am giving my school _____ minutes/hours of FREE TIME today so that I complete or reduce these tasks (again, 6 does not have to be the goal!):

_____   _____

_____   _____

_____   _____

I am giving myself _____ minutes/hours of ME TIME today to give myself time to relax/do something I enjoy (again, 6 does not have to be the goal):

_____   _____

_____   _____

_____   _____

ME TIME will be at   _____ _____ _____
these times: _____ _____ _____

The tasks I am doing for FAMILY/FRIENDS today are (I have given you space for 10 but you can do less!)

_____   _____

_____   _____

_____   _____

_____   _____

_____   _____

Write down 3 things that went well today:

_____

_____

_____

Write down 3 things I enjoyed today:

_____

_____

_____

What have I learned from today that will help me enjoy tomorrow?:

_____

_____

_____

DATE: _____

PLANNING AND JOURNALING!

In addition to my general TA duties today, I would like to complete or reduce these tasks (I've given you room to write 6 but please do not feel 6 is the goal unless you want it to be!):

_____   _____

_____   _____

_____   _____

I am giving my school _____ minutes/hours of FREE TIME today so that I complete or reduce these tasks (again, 6 does not have to be the goal!):

_____   _____

_____   _____

_____   _____

I am giving myself _____ minutes/hours of ME TIME today to give myself time to relax/do something I enjoy (again, 6 does not have to be the goal):

_____   _____

_____   _____

_____   _____

ME TIME will be at   _____ _____ _____
these times: _____ _____ _____

The tasks I am doing for FAMILY/FRIENDS today are (I have given you space for 10 but you can do less!)

_____   _____

_____   _____

_____   _____

_____   _____

_____   _____

Write down 3 things that went well today:

_____

_____

_____

Write down 3 things I enjoyed today:

_____

_____

_____

What have I learned from today that will help me enjoy tomorrow?:

_____

_____

_____

DATE: _____

PLANNING AND JOURNALING!

In addition to my general TA duties today, I would like to complete or reduce these tasks (I've given you room to write 6 but please do not feel 6 is the goal unless you want it to be!):

_____   _____

_____   _____

_____   _____

I am giving my school _____ minutes/hours of FREE TIME today so that I complete or reduce these tasks (again, 6 does not have to be the goal!):

_____   _____

_____   _____

_____   _____

I am giving myself _____ minutes/hours of ME TIME today to give myself time to relax/do something I enjoy (again, 6 does not have to be the goal):

_____   _____

_____   _____

_____   _____

ME TIME will be at these times: _____ _____ _____

_____ _____ _____

The tasks I am doing for FAMILY/FRIENDS today are (I have given you space for 10 but you can do less!)

_____   _____

_____   _____

_____   _____

_____   _____

_____   _____

Write down 3 things that went well today:

_____

_____

_____

Write down 3 things I enjoyed today:

_____

_____

_____

What have I learned from today that will help me enjoy tomorrow?:

_____

_____

_____

DATE: _____

PLANNING AND JOURNALING!

In addition to my general TA duties today, I would like to complete or reduce these tasks (I've given you room to write 6 but please do not feel 6 is the goal unless you want it to be!):

_____   _____

_____   _____

_____   _____

I am giving my school _____ minutes/hours of FREE TIME today so that I complete or reduce these tasks (again, 6 does not have to be the goal!):

_____   _____

_____   _____

_____   _____

I am giving myself _____ minutes/hours of ME TIME today to give myself time to relax/do something I enjoy (again, 6 does not have to be the goal):

_____   _____

_____   _____

_____   _____

ME TIME will be at   _____ _____ _____
these times: _____ _____ _____

The tasks I am doing for FAMILY/FRIENDS today are (I have given you space for 10 but you can do less!)

_____   _____

_____   _____

_____   _____

_____   _____

_____   _____

Write down 3 things that went well today:

_____

_____

_____

Write down 3 things I enjoyed today:

_____

_____

_____

What have I learned from today that will help me enjoy tomorrow?:

_____

_____

_____

DAY 23

DATE: _____

PLANNING AND JOURNALING!

In addition to my general TA duties today, I would like to complete or reduce these tasks (I've given you room to write 6 but please do not feel 6 is the goal unless you want it to be!):

_____   _____

_____   _____

_____   _____

I am giving my school _____ minutes/hours of FREE TIME today so that I complete or reduce these tasks (again, 6 does not have to be the goal!):

_____   _____

_____   _____

_____   _____

I am giving myself _____ minutes/hours of ME TIME today to give myself time to relax/do something I enjoy (again, 6 does not have to be the goal):

_____   _____

_____   _____

_____   _____

ME TIME will be at these times: _____ _____ _____

_____ _____ _____

The tasks I am doing for FAMILY/FRIENDS today are (I have given you space for 10 but you can do less!)

_____   _____

_____   _____

_____   _____

_____   _____

_____   _____

Write down 3 things that went well today:

_____

_____

_____

Write down 3 things I enjoyed today:

_____

_____

_____

What have I learned from today that will help me enjoy tomorrow?:

_____

_____

_____

DATE: _____

PLANNING AND JOURNALING!

In addition to my general TA duties today, I would like to complete or reduce these tasks (I've given you room to write 6 but please do not feel 6 is the goal unless you want it to be!):

_____   _____

_____   _____

_____   _____

I am giving my school _____ minutes/hours of FREE TIME today so that I complete or reduce these tasks (again, 6 does not have to be the goal!):

_____   _____

_____   _____

_____   _____

I am giving myself _____ minutes/hours of ME TIME today to give myself time to relax/do something I enjoy (again, 6 does not have to be the goal):

_____   _____

_____   _____

_____   _____

ME TIME will be at these times: _____ _____ _____

_____ _____ _____

The tasks I am doing for FAMILY/FRIENDS today are (I have given you space for 10 but you can do less!)

_____   _____

_____   _____

_____   _____

_____   _____

_____   _____

Write down 3 things that went well today:

_____

_____

_____

Write down 3 things I enjoyed today:

_____

_____

_____

What have I learned from today that will help me enjoy tomorrow?:

_____

_____

_____

DATE: _____

PLANNING AND JOURNALING!

In addition to my general TA duties today, I would like to complete or reduce these tasks (I've given you room to write 6 but please do not feel 6 is the goal unless you want it to be!):

_____   _____

_____   _____

_____   _____

I am giving my school _____ minutes/hours of FREE TIME today so that I complete or reduce these tasks (again, 6 does not have to be the goal!):

_____   _____

_____   _____

_____   _____

I am giving myself _____ minutes/hours of ME TIME today to give myself time to relax/do something I enjoy (again, 6 does not have to be the goal):

_____   _____

_____   _____

_____   _____

ME TIME will be at   _____ _____ _____
these times:
                            _____ _____ _____

The tasks I am doing for FAMILY/FRIENDS today are (I have given you space for 10 but you can do less!)

_____   _____

_____   _____

_____   _____

_____   _____

_____   _____

Write down 3 things that went well today:

_____

_____

_____

Write down 3 things I enjoyed today:

_____

_____

_____

What have I learned from today that will help me enjoy tomorrow?:

_____

_____

_____

DATE: _____

PLANNING AND JOURNALING!

In addition to my general TA duties today, I would like to complete or reduce these tasks (I've given you room to write 6 but please do not feel 6 is the goal unless you want it to be!):

_____   _____

_____   _____

_____   _____

I am giving my school _____ minutes/hours of FREE TIME today so that I complete or reduce these tasks (again, 6 does not have to be the goal!):

_____   _____

_____   _____

_____   _____

I am giving myself _____ minutes/hours of ME TIME today to give myself time to relax/do something I enjoy (again, 6 does not have to be the goal):

_____   _____

_____   _____

_____   _____

ME TIME will be at these times: _____ _____ _____

_____ _____ _____

The tasks I am doing for FAMILY/FRIENDS today are (I have given you space for 10 but you can do less!)

_____   _____

_____   _____

_____   _____

_____   _____

_____   _____

Write down 3 things that went well today:

_____

_____

_____

Write down 3 things I enjoyed today:

_____

_____

_____

What have I learned from today that will help me enjoy tomorrow?:

_____

_____

_____

_____

DATE: _____

PLANNING AND JOURNALING!

In addition to my general TA duties today, I would like to complete or reduce these tasks (I've given you room to write 6 but please do not feel 6 is the goal unless you want it to be!):

_____   _____

_____   _____

_____   _____

I am giving my school _____ minutes/hours of FREE TIME today so that I complete or reduce these tasks (again, 6 does not have to be the goal!):

_____   _____

_____   _____

_____   _____

I am giving myself _____ minutes/hours of ME TIME today to give myself time to relax/do something I enjoy (again, 6 does not have to be the goal):

_____   _____

_____   _____

_____   _____

ME TIME will be at   _____ _____ _____
these times: _____ _____ _____

The tasks I am doing for FAMILY/FRIENDS today are (I have given you space for 10 but you can do less!)

_____   _____

_____   _____

_____   _____

_____   _____

_____   _____

Write down 3 things that went well today:

_____

_____

_____

Write down 3 things I enjoyed today:

_____

_____

_____

What have I learned from today that will help me enjoy tomorrow?:

_____

_____

_____

DAY 28

PLANNING AND JOURNALING!

In addition to my general TA duties today, I would like to complete or reduce these tasks (I've given you room to write 6 but please do not feel 6 is the goal unless you want it to be!):

_____   _____

_____   _____

_____   _____

I am giving my school ____ minutes/hours of FREE TIME today so that I complete or reduce these tasks (again, 6 does not have to be the goal!):

_____   _____

_____   _____

_____   _____

I am giving myself ____ minutes/hours of ME TIME today to give myself time to relax/do something I enjoy (again, 6 does not have to be the goal):

_____   _____

_____   _____

_____   _____

ME TIME will be at these times: _____ _____ _____
_____ _____ _____

The tasks I am doing for FAMILY/FRIENDS today are (I have given you space for 10 but you can do less!)

_____   _____

_____   _____

_____   _____

_____   _____

_____   _____

Write down 3 things that went well today:

_____

_____

_____

Write down 3 things I enjoyed today:

_____

_____

_____

What have I learned from today that will help me enjoy tomorrow?:

_____

_____

_____

DATE: _____

PLANNING AND JOURNALING!

In addition to my general TA duties today, I would like to complete or reduce these tasks (I've given you room to write 6 but please do not feel 6 is the goal unless you want it to be!):

_____   _____

_____   _____

_____   _____

I am giving my school _____ minutes/hours of FREE TIME today so that I complete or reduce these tasks (again, 6 does not have to be the goal!):

_____   _____

_____   _____

_____   _____

I am giving myself _____ minutes/hours of ME TIME today to give myself time to relax/do something I enjoy (again, 6 does not have to be the goal):

_____   _____

_____   _____

_____   _____

ME TIME will be at
these times: _____ _____ _____

                      _____ _____ _____

The tasks I am doing for FAMILY/FRIENDS today are (I have given you space for 10 but you can do less!)

_____   _____

_____   _____

_____   _____

_____   _____

_____   _____

Write down 3 things that went well today:

_____

_____

_____

Write down 3 things I enjoyed today:

_____

_____

_____

What have I learned from today that will help me enjoy tomorrow?:

_____

_____

_____

DATE: _____

PLANNING AND JOURNALING!

In addition to my general TA duties today, I would like to complete or reduce these tasks (I've given you room to write 6 but please do not feel 6 is the goal unless you want it to be!):

_____   _____

_____   _____

_____   _____

I am giving my school _____ minutes/hours of FREE TIME today so that I complete or reduce these tasks (again, 6 does not have to be the goal!):

_____   _____

_____   _____

_____   _____

I am giving myself _____ minutes/hours of ME TIME today to give myself time to relax/do something I enjoy (again, 6 does not have to be the goal):

_____   _____

_____   _____

_____   _____

ME TIME will be at   _____ _____ _____
these times: _____ _____ _____

The tasks I am doing for FAMILY/FRIENDS today are (I have given you space for 10 but you can do less!)

_____   _____

_____   _____

_____   _____

_____   _____

_____   _____

Write down 3 things that went well today:

_____

_____

_____

Write down 3 things I enjoyed today:

_____

_____

_____

What have I learned from today that will help me enjoy tomorrow?:

_____

_____

_____

WHAT CHANGES WILL YOU MAKE ON A REGULAR BASIS NOW THAT YOU HAVE COMPLETED YOUR 30 DAYS OF PLANNING, JOURNALING, AND REFLECTING?

What went well over the last 30 days?

_____   _____

_____   _____

_____   _____

What went not so well over the last 30 days?

_____   _____

_____   _____

_____   _____

What can I do to improve the thing(s) that did not work so well?

_____

_____

_____

_____

_____

_____

WHAT COULD A TYPICAL DAY IN MY LIFE LOOK LIKE FROM NOW ON?

The work I do for money will start at _____ and end at _____

I will work _____ minutes/hours for free.

I will give myself _____ minutes/hours to do something I enjoy.

I will spend _____ minutes/hours doing things for/with my family.

I will spend _____ minutes/hours doing things for/with my friends.

Each day does not have to be spent on all of these. Just make sure that, overall, your week includes a healthy selection and includes time spent for yourself!

This is what I will do to increase my ENJOYMENT today:

_____

_____

_____

_____

EXPANDING THE TIME YOU ENJOY, CONTRACTING THE TIME YOU DON'T!

ENJOYING YOUR TIME!

Working your way through this book to create more time for yourself is NOT like being in school. You do not have to REMEMBER EVERYTHING and COMPLETE EVERY lesson!

If you're reading this page, it could be because you have studiously gone through every exercise or it might be that you have skimmed through it, taking what means something to you or it could be that you've skipped everything and found yourself here. Whichever of those fits you, that's fine!

The more you know about your use of time, through doing the exercises in this book, the more you will get from this section, but this section CAN be completed in isolation so if you're not great at completing exercises, you're STILL GOOD!

On the next few pages we will look at ways to INCREASE your ENJOYMENT of your work.

Now, before we get to that, I want to say that no amount of the following information in this section will help if you with work time if TOTALLY HATE your job!

ENJOYING YOUR TIME!

So, let me ask you that question:

'Do you hate your job?'

You'll know the answer immediately because you'll either feel a sensation that says 'No!' or you'll feel one that says 'Yes!'.

If 'Yes' is your answer then use some of the extra time you've gained from working on valuing and prioritising YOU time and FAMILY/FRIENDS time to explore what your new job/career will be.

But, if 'No!' is your answer...read on!

ENJOYING YOUR TIME!

BE LESS EVERYTHING TO EVERYONE AND DECIDE TO BE SOMETHING TO SOMEONE INSTEAD!

If you've been struggling with being a TA, and I'm guessing it could be one of the reasons you bought this book, then think very hard about how you want your future in this job to go.

We all see examples of DOING TOO MUCH leading to BURNOUT in others but we tend to deny it in ourselves.

So, ask yourself:

From the previous exercises, what have you learned about your job that will allow you to take your foot off the gas in some parts of it?

_____

_____

_____

_____

ENJOYING YOUR TIME!

BE LESS EVERYTHING TO EVERYONE AND DECIDE TO BE SOMETHING TO SOMEONE INSTEAD!

In what ways would your job improve if you decided NOT to be ALL THINGS TO EVERYONE?

_____

_____

_____

_____

Which tasks at work could you spend less time on?

_____

_____

_____

_____

ENJOYING YOUR TIME!

BE LESS EVERYTHING TO EVERYONE AND DECIDE TO BE SOMETHING TO SOMEONE INSTEAD!

Knowing that there will ALWAYS be work waiting for you, what time is your CUT OFF point for doing and/or thinking about your work?

_____

_____

_____

_____

_____

How will you foster independence from your help in some of the staff and children you support?

_____

_____

_____

_____

_____

ENJOYING YOUR TIME!

BE LESS EVERYTHING TO EVERYONE AND DECIDE TO BE SOMETHING TO SOMEONE INSTEAD!

Are there any members of staff you currently help that from now on you'll quietly leave to their own devices?

_____

_____

_____

_____

Are there any children you currently help that from now on you'll quietly leave to their own devices?

_____

_____

_____

_____

ENJOYING YOUR TIME!

DITCH THE DISAPPOINTMENT! UNDERSTAND AND ACCEPT THAT NO ONE IS PERFECT, NOT YOU AND NOT YOUR COLLEAGUES!

Once you understand that NO ONE is PERFECT, you'll FREE YOURSELF as well as your colleagues from that expectation.

Most of us do the BEST we can with what we have at the time. Sometimes that BEST is GREAT and other times, NOT SO great. When you STOP feeling disappointed in others, you'll be more FORGIVING to yourself.

So, ask yourself:

How much better would you feel if you didn't try to do EVERYTHING PERFECTLY?

_____

_____

_____

_____

ENJOYING YOUR TIME!

DITCH THE DISAPPOINTMENT! UNDERSTAND AND ACCEPT THAT NO ONE IS PERFECT, NOT YOU AND NOT YOUR COLLEAGUES!

How much better would you feel if you STOPPED trying to be a MODEL member of staff and REDUCED the FREE hours you give to school or stayed at home when you are ill?

_____

_____

_____

_____

_____

How much better would you feel if you ACCEPTED that most, if not all, of your colleagues are DOING THEIR BEST?

_____

_____

_____

_____

ENJOYING YOUR TIME!

DITCH THE DISAPPOINTMENT! UNDERSTAND AND ACCEPT THAT NO ONE IS PERFECT, NOT YOU AND NOT YOUR COLLEAGUES!

How much better would you feel if you ACCEPTED that schools are IMPERFECT places for IMPERFECT adults and children who are IMPERFECTLY trying their best?

_____

_____

_____

_____

(None of this means you let go of your aspiration of improvement and, of course, neglecting responsibilities is ALWAYS <u>unacceptable</u>, but when you understand that striving for improvement does not require you to strive for perfection, you improve FASTER!)

ENJOYING YOUR TIME!

FIND YOUR WHY!

EVERY job has aspects to it that are not enjoyable in and of themselves. So what you need to do here is look at WHY a particular task has to be done. THINK about the GOOD things that wouldn't happen if you didn't do certain tasks.

For example:

If nobody did playground duty the children wouldn't get VALUABLE time to exercise/get some fresh air/talk to their friends etc.

If you weren't there to support English lessons, some children would get further behind.

If you didn't spend time with that 'angry' child trying to show them how to reduce their temper, they'd have one less person they could trust.

If you didn't go to work, your family would have less money etc.

So, ask yourself:

ENJOYING YOUR TIME!

FIND YOUR WHY!

If I did not do (write it here)

what GOOD things WOULDN'T HAPPEN?

_____

_____

If I did not do (write it here)

what GOOD things WOULDN'T HAPPEN?

_____

_____

If I did not do (write it here)

what GOOD things WOULDN'T HAPPEN?

_____

_____

ENJOYING YOUR TIME!

FIND YOUR WHY!

If I did not do (write it here)

what GOOD things WOULDN'T HAPPEN?

_____

_____

If I did not do (write it here)

what GOOD things WOULDN'T HAPPEN?

_____

_____

If I did not do (write it here)

what GOOD things WOULDN'T HAPPEN?

_____

_____

ENJOYING YOUR TIME!

SEE TAKING A BREAK AS A WAY OF BEING <u>MORE</u> PRODUCTIVE, <u>NOT</u> LESS!

Schools have become places where NOT taking a break is worn like a BADGE of HONOUR.

But, there is NOTHING HONOURABLE about NOT TAKING A BREAK!

Ten minutes of sitting with a cuppa and connecting with a colleague, is ten minutes WELL SPENT because it will enable you to be BETTER than you would have been without it.

And, the thing is: YOU are a TEACHING ASSISTANT. YOU are NOT the TEACHER! THAT has a DISTINCT ADVANTAGE because you DO NOT HAVE ALL THE RESPONSIBILITY, so TAKE A BREAK!

It DOES NOT MATTER that some of your colleagues don't. That is up to them!

If YOU TAKE a BREAK, you'll be in a BETTER position to HANDLE any difficulties that come your way!

Ask yourself:

ENJOYING YOUR TIME!

SEE TAKING A BREAK AS A WAY OF BEING <u>MORE</u> PRODUCTIVE, <u>NOT</u> LESS!

How can you organise your days, when you have no duties at breaktime, to take a break at breaktime?

_____

_____

_____

_____

How can you organise your days when you are not required to cover at lunchtime to take a break at lunchtime?

_____

_____

_____

_____

ENJOYING YOUR TIME!

SEE TAKING A BREAK AS A WAY OF BEING <u>MORE</u> PRODUCTIVE, <u>NOT</u> LESS!

What tasks can you build into your day that give you some space away from the busy classroom? (i.e. going to the resource area to replenish classroom resources, working on a display in the corridor, looking for lost uniform etc).

_____

_____

_____

_____

_____

_____

_____

_____

ENJOYING YOUR TIME!

NEUTRALIZE NEGATIVITY WHEREVER YOU GO!

It's so easy to get caught up in negativity. It's also very understandable. BUT, negativity breeds more negativity and BEFORE you know it, you're feeling frustrated, irritated, angry, uninspired, anxious and a bit down on a DAILY BASIS.

The way to remedy this is to CHECK IN with your thoughts and UP-LEVEL them from low-level thinking that generally predicts poor outcomes to a higher-level of thought that isn't so positive that you dismiss it as unobtainable but instead it's realistic and in alignment with WHO YOU ARE.

Negative thoughts disguise themselves as the truth. They appear as the negative side of 'all or nothing' type thoughts.

So, when you believe you don't know enough, you're not good enough or something won't work, for instance, these thoughts are the negatives to believing you do know enough, you are good enough and something will work.

ENJOYING YOUR TIME!

NEUTRALIZE NEGATIVITY WHEREVER YOU GO!

But there's so much more to making decisions than yes or no, it will or it won't or it is or it isn't, because between yes and no, it will or it won't or it is or it isn't, are a host of other possibilities.

Something might go from a no to a yes, if something else is done. Something could go from a won't to a will if you get some help. And something might go from it isn't to it is, if you get some more information.

To find the other possibilities, you have to look for the realistic thoughts that take into account who you are and what you know rather than closing down your possibilities with an all or nothing type answer.

Here's how you do that...

Take a thought like:

'Oh, I wish I didn't have to support English this morning, it's going to feel like wading through treacle!'

ENJOYING YOUR TIME!

NEUTRALIZE NEGATIVITY WHEREVER YOU GO!

Next, think of the exact opposite of that thought:

'Oh, I'm so looking forward to supporting English this morning, it's going to feel wonderful!'

And then think of a couple of realistic possibilities that fall between the negative and the positive thought, such as:

'I know supporting English isn't my favourite thing to do but if I focus on helping the teacher, I think that will be a better use of my time'   Or...

'I know I feel a sense of dread about supporting English but if I get a good understanding of what is being taught beforehand, I'll feel a greater sense of achievement'

Do you see how that works? It's NOT about being overly POSITIVE, it's about coming up with thoughts that are in ALIGNMENT with YOU that are neither negative or so positive you believe they're not possible for you.

ENJOYING YOUR TIME!

NEUTRALIZE NEGATIVITY WHEREVER YOU GO!

Here's some REALISTIC THOUGHT CREATOR practice for you:

Write down 1 thought about something you are feeling negatively about (this is a negative thought):

_____

_____

Next, write down the EXACT OPPOSITE of the above thought (this is an overly positive thought):

_____

_____

Then, write down two thoughts that fall between the negative and positive and are in alignment with who you are (these are realistic thoughts):

_____

_____

_____

_____

ENJOYING YOUR TIME!

NEUTRALIZE NEGATIVITY WHEREVER YOU GO!

Keep practicing!:

Write down 1 thought about something you are feeling negatively about (this is a negative thought):

_____

_____

Next, write down the EXACT OPPOSITE of the above thought (this is an overly positive thought):

_____

_____

Then, write down two thoughts that fall between the negative and positive and are in alignment with who you are (these are realistic thoughts):

_____

_____

_____

_____

ENJOYING YOUR TIME!

NEUTRALIZE NEGATIVITY WHEREVER YOU GO!

Keep practicing!:

Write down 1 thought about something you are feeling negatively about (this is a negative thought):

_____

_____

Next, write down the EXACT OPPOSITE of the above thought (this is an overly positive thought):

_____

_____

Then, write down two thoughts that fall between the negative and positive and are in alignment with who you are (these are realistic thoughts):

_____

_____

_____

_____

ENJOYING YOUR TIME!

NEUTRALIZE NEGATIVITY WHEREVER YOU GO!

Keep practicing!:

Write down 1 thought about something you are feeling negatively about (this is a negative thought):

_____

_____

Next, write down the EXACT OPPOSITE of the above thought (this is an overly positive thought):

_____

_____

Then, write down two thoughts that fall between the negative and positive and are in alignment with who you are (these are realistic thoughts):

_____

_____

_____

_____

ENJOYING YOUR TIME!

NEUTRALIZE NEGATIVITY WHEREVER YOU GO!

Keep practicing!:

Write down 1 thought about something you are feeling negatively about (this is a negative thought):

_____

_____

Next, write down the EXACT OPPOSITE of the above thought (this is an overly positive thought):

_____

_____

Then, write down two thoughts that fall between the negative and positive and are in alignment with who you are (these are realistic thoughts):

_____

_____

_____

_____

ENJOYING YOUR TIME!

Hopefully, through practicing this, you are beginning to see that there are many possibilities between the negative and the overly positive and that all or nothing thinking will become a thing of the past for you.

Finding, at least SOME ENJOYMENT during your day where you BELIEVED there was NONE can only EVER be a GOOD THING for you!

To summarize this section:

You can EXPAND your ENJOYMENT of your time in school by doing the following...

1) Ditching the disappointment of yourself and your colleagues by accepting that no one is perfect! This is a good thing, because when you do that you cut yourself, and others, some slack. Cutting some slack gives you more scope for trying new things rather than sticking rigidly to stuff that doesn't work for you.

2) Being less everything to everyone, because going down that route spreads your abilities way too thin

ENJOYING YOUR TIME!

and you end up not doing anything well. Decide which things you can do well and give most of your focus to those. It's about deciding which of the things you're currently doing, you're only doing because you THINK you have to!

3) Finding your why, because this will help you gain satisfaction in the tasks you don't particularly enjoy. Knowing the good things that would not happen if you did not do a particular task, will increase your ability to get it done with a good heart!

4) Taking a break, because it is necessary for good mental health. Taking a break will help you to stay on an even keel and it will enable you to help others better!

5) Neutralizing negativity will not only help you to find enjoyment where you believed there was none but it will also give you more energy. Negativity, whether it's your own or others, is a real energy thief!

All of these ENJOYMENT EXPANDERS will help you move through your day with more of a SPRING in your step!

Time spent on pulling together what you've learned will make change possible!

PULLING IT ALL TOGETHER!

The aim of this book was to help you move on from just wishing you had more time to seeing that techniques and strategies exist to help time expand or contract.

This is possible because of the way the human brain works i.e. when we are enjoying something time feels expansive and passes quickly but when we are not enjoying something time feels rigid and drags.

So, in this book I have given you strategies to experience more enjoyment in your day, by LEARNING how to VALUE your time, PRIORITISE your time, REFLECT on how you use your time and UNDERSTAND how to EXPAND your ENJOYMENT of time.

NONE of this is ROCKET SCIENCE and NONE of it is about waving a MAGIC WAND to make everything all right.

If there is something in your life that is making you MISERABLE, that thing HAS TO CHANGE before the strategies and techniques in this book can be of service to you.

PULLING IT ALL TOGETHER!

To imagine that the strategies and techniques in this book can somehow make everything okay for you when currently there's something BIG making you UNHAPPY, is a mistake.

It's like expecting a child who hates school to suddenly like school because you've told them school is great! You have to first find out what their underlying anxieties are and help them to feel safe before any progress can be made, and it's the same for you!

However, the strategies and techniques in this book can make a BIG DIFFERENCE for you if your work life is basically good and it's just that it could be better!

Reading this book and deploying the strategies and techniques in THIS SITUATION is like teaching children who are ready to learn, because they will absorb new information, apply what they've learned and make progress.

As with all new knowledge, you will need to re-read it and practice it. It's common amongst humans to be all fired up about something one minute and then move

PULLING IT ALL TOGETHER!

on to something else the next, because the effort to make change seems too great. But, EFFORT is ALWAYS required to make change, so let me ask you this...

Which scenario would you prefer?:

To be enjoying more of your time in school in 3 months from now because you've made some effort and deployed a couple of strategies and techniques. You haven't done this perfectly but you are now getting better at it and can see how deploying more strategies and techniques will benefit you.   Or...

To still be wishing you had more time in school in 3 months from now and still on the look out for the thing that will make all the difference to you.

I know which one of these I would prefer. And the thing is...the thing that will make all the difference to you, IS YOU! SO, <u>BE</u> THE DIFFERENCE you want to CREATE!

It boils down to how much time you want to spend searching for the NONE EXISTENT GOLDEN NUGGET that somehow turns things around rather than

PULLING IT ALL TOGETHER!

getting on with turning things around NOW!

Like you, and ALL of us, NO system, technique or strategy is PERFECT, but as you've learned in this book, if you didn't know it already, something DOESN'T have to be PERFECT in order to WORK!

So, set about IMPERFECTLY trying out the strategies and techniques in this book to find out which of them IMPERFECTLY work for you!

If one of them works, then that's one technique or strategy you can use that you didn't have before.

And if ONE works, there's a GOOD chance MORE THAN ONE WILL WORK!

But, NONE of them will work if you close this book and never open it again.

You DON'T HAVE TO believe in yourself and you DON'T HAVE TO believe in this book. Because, to CREATE CHANGE, ALL YOU HAVE TO DO is TAKE SOME IMPERFECT ACTION!

ABOUT THE AUTHOR!

Hello there, I'm Lauren Riesner and I help Teaching Assistants with their daily routines, mindset, the interview process and much much more...

I live in Devon in Southwest England with my husband Tim and my 2 mad springers, Boy and Freya and I create books that are tailor-made for Teaching Assistants.

Having previously been a TA/HLTA/1:1 TA for 20 years, I've noticed that there isn't very much out there for Teaching Assistants to improve your working routines, to support your teaching or to assist you with the challenges of behaviour, intervention sessions, subject knowledge etc.

My writing is all about improvement and my books are written with the intention to make the job of TA easier. Being a Teaching Assistant can be tough and so many of you make a huge effort for the children you work with and you ask for so little in return. Think of my books as friendly helping hands and use them to help you work smarter rather than even harder!

I am a one woman set up. I do not have a publishing team to proof-read my books or to edit them and set them out so that everything looks symmetrical etc. I do all this myself and because of that, you may detect the odd typo, missing punctuation or misalignment of text etc.

I keep the prices of my books at a level that I hope Teaching Assistants can afford, but again, because I am not part of a bigger machine it is impossible for me to place my books at a super-low price.

I pay Amazon to print and deliver my books which means I earn somewhere between £1-£3 for every book sold, depending on the price I've set it at.

EVERY book I write is written with the intention of supporting TAs with your work. I hope this book fulfils that intention for you. But, whether it does or doesn't, I'd appreciate you leaving me a written review. Good or not so good, your review will give me vital information that will allow me to improve this book for TAs in the future.

Much love,

Lauren Riesner

AND FINALLY...

Thank you for buying this book, I truly hope it has enhanced your ability to be the best TA you can be. Having been a TA/HLTA myself for 20 years, I'm on a mission to support you in whatever ways I can.

I have MANY more TA books. Below is just a selection. To see them all either type the url below into your browser or copy the QR code:

STAY ONE STEP AHEAD IN ENGLISH AND MATHS:

GET THE EDGE ON YOUR COMPETITION AT INTERVIEW:

PLAN, TRACK AND ASSESS YOUR INTERVENTION SESSIONS:

taincontrol.com/BOOKS

SMASH YOUR NEGATIVE THOUGHTS:

SMASHING PLANNERS:

REMEMBER EVERYTHING WITH TO DO LIST NOTEBOOKS:

COPY THIS QR CODE TO SEE ALL OF MY BOOKS: